IRELAND 1945-70

IRELAND
1945-70

Edited by J. J. Lee

Thomas Davis Lectures

GILL AND MACMILLAN, DUBLIN
BARNES & NOBLE BOOKS, NEW YORK
a division of Harper & Row Publishers, Inc.

First published 1979 by
Gill and Macmillan Ltd
15/17 Eden Quay
Dublin 1
with associated companies in
London, New York, Delhi, Hong Kong,
Johannesburg, Lagos, Melbourne,
Singapore, Tokyo

0 7171 0943 7

Published in the U.S.A. 1980 by
Harper & Row Publishers, Inc.
Barnes & Noble Import Division

ISBN 0 – 06 – 494129 – 9

Library of Congress Catalog Number:
LC 79 – 53791

Printed in Great Britain by
Bristol Typesetting Co. Ltd., Barton Manor, St Philips, Bristol

Contents

Contents continued

Preface

Thirteen of the fourteen essays in this book were originally broadcast as a series of Thomas Davis Lectures on Radio Eireann in 1978. An additional essay on Northern Ireland by Dr Cornelius O'Leary has been included in this volume. The book deals with a more recent period of Irish history than any comparable volume in the Thomas Davis series, and the contributors were faced with problems of perspective and evidence in what is in some respects a pioneer venture. Nevertheless, the volume attempts to interpret in an incisive and informed manner developments across a wide range of Irish life, including politics, economics, education, religion, culture, the media, and the environment.

The general editor of the Thomas Davis Lecture series was Michael Lyttleton of RTE. I am greatly indebted to him for his unfailing encouragement and constructive criticism at all stages of the planning and production of the series. The publishers assumed the burden of seeing this volume of re-written essays through the press. That it appears so relatively soon after the original series of broadcasts is eloquent tribute to their skill and tenacity in surmounting the hazards of co-operative scholarship.

J. J. Lee
February 1979

'Put them out!'
Parties and Elections, 1948-69

John A. Murphy

'Let Lemass Lead On'. 'Back Jack'. 'The Just Society'. 'The Seventies will be Socialist'. The slogan has always been an essential part of the Irish election scene but the anti-Fianna Fáil rallying cry in 1948—'Put Them Out'—had unusually forceful connotations and, in the event, a particularly telling effect. 'They', the slogan was meant to convey, had been in power for far too long—an uninterrupted sixteen years of office—had grown old, tired and arrogant and, it was hinted, corrupt into the bargain. Besides, since the political face of Britain and Europe was being rapidly transformed, was it not high time for a change here also?

Who was to be 'put in', however, was far from clear. There was certainly no sign of an anti-Fianna Fáil common front. After its disastrous losses in 1943, Fine Gael appeared to be a dwindling minority party rather than an alternative government: when W. T. Cosgrave had retired from the leadership in January 1944, his successor Richard Mulcahy was at that time without a Dáil seat. Labour was in industrial and political schism and could not, in any event, hope to benefit from the post-war desire for change : unlike its British brother, it was in no position to offer, still less deliver, anything like a welfare state. Clann na Talmhan had been a regional and sectional party from the outset, and by 1948 was already experiencing the classic difficulties besetting a farmers' political organisation.

It was a new party, then, which dramatically threw down the gauntlet in 1948 and which cherished the greatest expectations of being 'put in'. I have dealt elsewhere[1] with the rise and fall of Clann na Poblachta, perhaps the most interesting phenomenon in the history of the state. Here I should like to add a comment on its policies. The party is sometimes thought of as having been 'radical' which in turn is equated with 'socialist'. This is a misconception. 'Radical' Clann na Poblachta certainly was, in the sense that it sought national and social regeneration. But the banner it raised was similar to that which had once been zestfully borne by Fianna Fáil. To the extent that the new party had a blueprint of its own, it was less influenced by socialism than by Catholic social principles and the new vogue for Christian democracy in Europe. Indeed, it is an anachronism to think that any party seriously bidding for power in the clericalist Ireland of 1948 could have run on a socialist ticket. The young men who flocked into Clann na Poblachta in 1946 and 1947 were doubtless interested in what was happening in welfare state Britain but Irish social idealism had to be decked out in suitably respectable clothes. Thus, the party election posters promised the implementation of Bishop Dignan's social insurance plan (summarily rejected by Fianna Fáil) and, more generally, envisaged the building of a 'social and economic system based on Christian principles'.[2]

The high hopes of Clann na Poblachta in 1948 were reflected in its decision to put forward over ninety candidates.[3] Accordingly, the poor performance of the party in winning only ten seats was a shattering disappointment that had much wider repercussions. It had set out to smash the seemingly permanent moulds of the so-called 'two-and-a-half' party system. When it failed to do so, the dice were more loaded than ever against any new parties that might be formed in the future. Yet, Clann na Poblachta played a significant role in Irish politics by interrupting Fianna Fáil monopoly, by helping to provide the electorate with a new choice between Fianna Fáil and coalition and, ironically in view of its republican wellsprings, by unwittingly giving the kiss of life to Fine Gael.

Fianna Fáil was 'put out' in 1948 by an extraordinary post-election coalition of its opponents, who now forgot their campaign antagonisms towards one another in a common reforming zeal and, more importantly, in a common resolve to 'keep them out'. Generally speaking, coalition benefited the larger parties at the expense of the smaller. While Clann na Poblachta was a spent force by 1951 and Clann na Talmhan was to peter out over the next decade into a nominal existence, Labour was enabled to paper over its cracks and Fine Gael experienced a phenomenal revival. That party was rescued from apparently imminent extinction by the prestige and self-confidence it derived from major participation in government. Its percentage of the popular vote climbed from just under 20 per cent in 1948 to 25.7 per cent in 1951, and to 32 per cent in 1954 : correspondingly its Dáil seats increased from 31 to 40 to 50.[4] Though the party suffered a sharp setback with the strong swing to Fianna Fáil in 1957, it could still face the future with some confidence and its Dáil strength was close to 50 throughout the 1960s. The resurgence of Fine Gael after 1948 merits Scotty Reston's memorable description of Richard Nixon's unexpected return to the centre of American politics, 'the greatest comeback since Lazarus'.

The 1950s and 1960s are two sharply contrasting periods, in respect of the economy and of Irish society generally. Truly, it was the worst of decades followed by the best of decades. The depression of the 1950s is reflected, as it were, in its electoral history. The general elections of 1951 and 1954 were lack-lustre affairs, and the changes of government a dreary see-saw.

The first inter-party administration collapsed in May 1951 and though Fianna Fáil increased its first preference vote by an impressive 4.4 per cent, it gained only one extra seat because of the new factor of inter-party transfers. Mr de Valera became Taoiseach again only with the help of some Independent deputies and entered upon his most undistinguished term of office. By-election defeats early in 1954 were the prelude to a loss of four Fianna Fáil seats in the general election of that year, and the party was reduced to its lowest Dáil strength since 1927. The second coalition (1954–57) comprised fewer parties than the first. John A. Costello became an inter-party Taoiseach for the second time and his role on this occasion tended to be less 'chairman' and more 'chief', to use Brian Farrell's useful classification.[5] But the economic and psychological gloom did not lift. Economic problems were compounded by political ones as the IRA mounted a cross-border campaign. The second coalition perished in 1957 in a sea of troubles.

An interesting, if minor, feature of the March 1957 election was the reappearance of Sinn Féin, the political wing of the IRA, entering the lists for the first time since 1927. Securing 66,000 first preferences and four seats, it was the obvious beneficiary of some popular support for the IRA campaign and of a wave of sympathy on the deaths of Sean South and Fergal O hAnnluain. But the sympathy was transient, and when Sinn Féin TDs displayed their traditional contempt for 'Leinster House' by refusing to sit there, a pragmatic electorate made sure the next time round that they would have *no* seats to reject.

However, the central issue of the 1957 general election was the bleak economic situation which in the mid-1950s had induced the most profound national despondency. Out of the depths of despair, there now came a significant swing to Fianna Fáil of 5 per cent, giving the party seventy-eight seats, its largest number to date, and a very comfortable overall majority. The new government was thus given a strong mandate to deal with the economy : given the ambivalent popular mood on the IRA, the result can hardly be interpreted as reflecting any great concern on the electorate's part with what later came to be called 'security'. Nevertheless, Fianna Fáil now proceeded to use its position of strength to deal as firmly, if not as harshly, with the IRA as it had done in the 1940s.

The rapid transformation of the economy and indeed of Irish society as a whole in the late 1950s and early 1960s constitutes a decisive turning point in the history of the Irish state. In a sense, politics remained the one static area in a period of widespread change, since the party system remained essentially the same. Yet party policies and personnel mirrored some of the vitality of that golden dawn. The greatest benefit, both in the short and long term, accrued to Fianna Fáil since they could plausibly claim that it was *their* programme for economic expansion that had *created* the new prosperity. The voters did not enquire too deeply into the global causes of capitalist slumps and booms. It was simpler to reduce economic complexities to domestic swings and roundabouts, so who could blame the average punter for thinking, as he increasingly did, that he always had a bob in his pocket when Fianna Fáil were in power?

One of the contrasts between the politics of the 1950s and 1960s was the noticeable change in dramatis personae. James Dillon succeeded Richard Mulcahy as leader of Fine Gael in 1959 but this was hardly a generational change. Both in terms of family background and florid parliamentary style, the ebullient Dillon was a throwback to the days of the old Irish party. Liam Cosgrave who took over from Dillon in 1965 represented all that was safe and conservative in Fine Gael : because he was profoundly influenced by his father, he was prone to the backward look, with a particular predilection for law and order and an inherent distrust of the forces of change within the party. Brendan Corish who, like Cosgrave, had served in the second coalition, replaced William Norton in 1960 as leader of Labour. Norton had led that party for almost thirty years, his early socialism mellowing to moderate reformism. Neither was his successor a socialist zealot[6] but the Corishes were solid and respected Wexford political stock and the new Labour leader was to retain a personal popularity with the party during its recurrent and well-publicised crises.

But it was in Fianna Fáil that leadership change was of the *most* interest. To many of the faithful, Hamlet without the Prince would have seemed a resounding box-office success compared with the prospects for their party's future without its founder. And yet the unthinkable had to be thought. In 1959, Eamon de Valera was seventy-seven years old, and heroically striving to cope with almost total blindness. He realised that the time had finally come for him to leave active politics. The circumstances of his last hurrah will be dealt with later: it is enough to say here that his departure for the living pantheon of the Presidency ended the role of Sean Lemass as his understudy.

Because of the long wait, Lemass's tenure of office as Taoiseach and leader of the Fianna Fáil party was brief (1959-66) but of the highest significance in a period of rapid change. The dominant political personality of the 1960s, he was as undisputed a ruler as 'the Chief' had ever been, but his own soubriquet of 'the Boss' aptly suggests the change in leadership style. His pragmatic, managerial talents won him the support of erstwhile unfriendly forces, for example, that of the *Cork Examiner* newspaper, hitherto Fine Gael-orientated. He led Fianna Fáil into two general elections: in 1961 the party secured less than an overall majority, yet such was the buoyancy of the times and the vigour of Lemass's rule that his minority government over the next four years, supported by some Independents, is commonly adjudged to have been one of the best in the history of the state. The 1965 election campaign was built around the slogan 'Let Lemass lead on', and the result was another Fianna Fáil government, this time with a slight working majority.

The Lemass years showed that Fianna Fáil could survive and thrive without Eamon de Valera : Lemass had been the power behind the throne well before the 'Chief' had retired and he had pulled the party out of the doldrums in the early 1950s. The change in party personnel which had been real but not very noticeable in the late 1950s was accelerated under Lemass and encouraged by him. The old warriors were gradually replaced : in the phraseology of the political scientists, the revolutionary elite gave place to the post-revolutionary elite.[7] De Valera's last administration in 1957 was still dominated by founder members of the party, though it included such new men as Jack Lynch, Neil Blaney, Kevin Boland and Michael Moran. Up to 1965, Lemass kept on in his cabinets such senior members as Dr Jim Ryan, Sean MacEntee and Frank Aiken but there was a further infusion of new blood with the introduction of Dr Paddy Hillery, C. J. Haughey and Brian Lenihan. The rejuvenation process was completed in 1965 : the durable Frank Aiken, de Valera's *fidus Achates*, was now *Oisín i ndiaidh na Féinne*, and George Colley, Donogh O'Malley, Joe Brennan and Sean Flanagan were given cabinet posts. It may be noted that the ministerial transition was from the old to the young. The persistence of the revolutionary group into the early 1960s gave no chance to the middle generation with the exception of one or two, such as Erskine Childers.

While Lemass, to use his own words, 'made changes . . . to make it quite clear to any new man that if he showed he had ability the road to promotion was fairly open to him',[8] he nevertheless made no attempt to groom any particular successor. This would, in any case, have been invidious as his son-in-law, Charles J. Haughey, was not deficient in ambition. So, Lemass's resignation in November 1966 gave rise to the first contest for leadership in Fianna Fáil since the foundation of the party forty years before. Haughey, Colley and Blaney were all interested but there was a strong groundswell of support for the Minister for Finance, Jack Lynch. Not only was Lynch senior to, and more experienced than the other contenders but he appealed as being likely to transcend the factions which they represented. This view was vindicated when Colley alone offered a challenge, to be soundly beaten by Lynch in the parliamentary party contest by fifty-one votes to nineteen. Accordingly the quietly spoken and pipe-smoking Corkman took over as leader of the party and as Taoiseach.

Handsome, genial and popular—the first Fianna Fáil leader with the truly common touch—Lynch's prowess in Gaelic games in the 1940s had eased his path, in classic Irish style, to a successful political career. Moving smoothly up the *cursus honorum* of government office, perhaps his greatest asset was an apparent lack of overweening ambition, so that he gave the impression of gracefully accepting the greatness that was thrust upon him rather than ruthlessly seeking it out. Unlike some of his rivals, he could not boast of a prominent republican family background but this was not necessarily a liability at a period when nationalism seemed dated. Lynch had no clearcut political philosophy and lacked Lemass's vigorous and innovative temperament. It does not seem unfair to say that he personified the party's development as it moved into the late 1960s, standing for nothing in particular except a kind of affable consensus.

In all three parties, then, the illusion of political change was provided by new leadership and personnel but it is questionable if there was any fundamental transformation in policies. Both constitutionally and socio-economically, Fine Gael and Fianna Fáil had long since been converging, and one of Fine Gael's main problems was to establish that it had some *raison d'être* other than being anti-Fianna Fáil. The conservative establishment within the party was loath to turn its back on its traditional supporters, the large farmers and the old 'respectable' middle class (for the snobs still saw Fine Gael as the 'nicer' of the two main parties). However, the young tigers—or fox cubs, as a subsequent hunting parlance would have it—sought to direct Fine Gael towards social democracy. Children of their generation, they shared the intense social concern of the 1960s, and their attempt to give the party a new conscience was as much influenced by a genuine desire to build a Just Society, as they termed it, as by political ambition and a determination to revitalise Fine Gael. The progressive group, led by Declan Costello, son of the former Coalition Taoiseach, was successful to the extent of having *The Just Society* accepted as party policy before the 1965 election but the lack of enthusiasm for it among the Fine Gael elders was obvious. (The proposal to adopt a new name, 'Social Democratic Party', was overwhelmingly defeated.) Tensions about leadership and policy continued to exist up to the end of our period though Fine Gael was much too sedate to experience anything so vulgar as a split. In terms of organisation, however, there was some improvement, and some modification, too, of the party's part-time and amateur character.

Concern about social injustice in a prospering society which animated the young progressives in Fine Gael was expressed in more acute form in other political areas. For the first time since the days of the Republican Congress in the 1930s, the IRA, through its political wing, Sinn Féin, became involved in social agitation, directed at such targets as inadequate housing and private control of fisheries. Inside parliament, the Irish social conscience was vigorously prodded by an evergreen radical, Dr Noel Browne, who with Jack McQuillan, an old comrade from Clann na Poblachta days, had founded the National Progressive Democrats in 1958. But it remained a two-man group in the Dáil until the admission of Browne and McQuillan to the Labour Party in 1963 when the NPD was dissolved. The strong and sustained opposition from within Labour to Browne's admission was due partly to doubts about his allegiance, in the light of a remarkably erratic political career, but largely to the problem posed by his undiluted socialism. For the controversy over Browne's admission raised a rather new dilemma for Irish Labour, namely, that of accommodating people like Browne, on the one hand, and on the other, the conservative and traditional-minded rural deputies who had independent power bases, who were little impressed by the recent vogue for socialism, even if Pope John had made it respectable, and whose own concept of socialism was little more than good neighbourliness of the St Vincent de Paul Society type. The dilemma became more acute as the 1960s wore on and Labour began to attract the kind of urban intellectual socialist who, up to then, had not seen the party as a congenial home. Like the young progressives in Fine Gael, the socialists in Labour *apparently* got their way against their conservative colleagues, in that their philosophy was adopted as party policy. But as in Fine Gael, the victory was an illusory one. The New Republic[9] was likewise greeted with a singular lack of enthusiasm by old Labour hands. It is easy, with hindsight, to suggest that Brendan Corish's best course would have been to expel from the parliamentary party all those not fully committed to socialism. But Labour was too small and weak to afford the luxury of such a purge which might well have resulted in a split, similar to the disastrous one of 1943.

Fianna Fáil's uninterrupted run of power in the 1960s owed something to the collapse of the coalition idea, as illustrated in the significant lack of preference transfers between Fine Gael and Labour in the elections of that decade. To the electors, it seemed that no alternative government was available. Labour was conscious of having gained little except junior office from previous coalitions and, as socialist ideology gained favour, was increasingly determined to go it alone. But a more positive factor in Fianna Fáil's success was its apparent party unity: the leadership contest in 1966 was its only open show of difference, though the first ominous rumblings of a later and more dramatic dissent became evident in early 1969 when Neil Blaney more than once expressed a view on the incipient Northern crisis which was at variance with that of the party leader. By and large, however, up to the end of our period at least, very little of the party's dirty linen was ever washed in public.

With respect to policy, Fianna Fáil had little difficulty in adapting itself, chameleon-like, to the changing scene in the 1960s. It made sufficient concessions, as in the sphere of education, to take the sharp edge off the hunger for greater justice and equality in Irish society, but went no further than that. To borrow a cynical teaching metaphor, it stayed a page ahead of the class. It became more than ever an amorphous, 'catch-all' and 'cross-class' party: for example, it was not adversely affected by the growing urbanisation of Irish society. An April 1969 Gallup survey[10] showed a strikingly wide distribution of Fianna Fáil support in terms of social class, region and age. It maintained its hold on the men of *little* property while becoming increasingly involved with the men of very *considerable* property that the Lemass era had attracted to the party's support. Such support took a substantial financial form and was openly organised in the mid-1960s in the shape of Taca—an auxiliary fund-raising association where big businessmen paid a large entrance

fee. The unusual and American-style developments evoked considerable criticism from the media and even from some of the
party faithful. Though defended then as now by Fianna Fáil
leaders as a perfectly legitimate operation, Taca was nevertheless seen to be a strategic error and silently faded away, at least
as an open organisation.[11]

The new political elite in the party took on the smooth image
of the swinging sixties. The rough and simple virtues of the
founding fathers now belonged to a remote age. As the mohair
suit replaced the legendary seatless trousers, the soldiers of
destiny became the self-confessed party of reality while still
managing to project the image of being the truly 'national'
party. But reference to the First Aims was more and more a
matter for occasional ritual reference. There was a revealing
moment on television during the Easter Rising anniversary
celebrations in 1966 when, on a platform outside the General
Post Office in Dublin, the ageing President de Valera spoke
of his dreams of a united Ireland and a revived language while
behind him his young successors listened uneasily to this em-
barrassing reminder of their origins.

Lively political columns became a regular newspaper feature
of the 1960s[12] and in the same decade television introduced an
altogether new and complicating factor into Irish politics. Good
television dramatised politics, political programmes stimulated
public interest and at election times there was considerable
publicity for politicians. But 'the box' was not always flattering
to those politicians who were trained in the chapel-gate tradition;
they were uneasy with a medium which made its election debut
only in 1965, and television exposure was soon seen to be a
double-edged sword. Politicians were slow to learn that the
medium demanded professional techniques from them. At the
same time, they resented the idea that they had to explain
themselves in front of the cameras which however they found
could not be ignored. Critical comment from a television station
operating under a public authority was highly unwelcome to
those in power, and Seán Lemass gave warning of the limits
that would be tolerated when he uttered his celebrated statement about television being 'an instrument of public policy'.[13]

On the whole, government distrusted the medium and tried
to keep the new opinion formers under control. In the nature

of things, governments—in our period, the Fianna Fáil government— had more to fear from television than had the opposition. Though there was no open clash in the 1960s between
the government and the new 'estate', the shape of things to
come was prefigured during the PR referendum campaign of
1968. Two well-known political scientists, Professor Basil Chubb
and Dr David Thornley, suggested in a television programme
that the introduction of the straight vote, which was being
proposed by Fianna Fáil for the second time in a decade, was
likely to give that party over 100 Dáil seats. The Chubb-
Thornley projection aroused considerable interest and, it was
commonly believed, helped to secure the decisive popular rejection of the government's proposal. The incident was an
interesting illustration of how television could influence a political
event, though it is difficult to determine whether and how
television significantly affected voting behaviour in general.

It may be added that television pundits themselves were
not immune from the fascination of politics. Some of them
abandoned the sideline for the playing field and their public
images achieved for them a fleeting popularity at the polls.

From 1948 to 1969 inclusive, there were seven general elections
(the average parliamentary life-span since 1923 of over three
years being maintained in our period), two contested presidential
elections—Fianna Fáil's Seán T. Ó Ceallaigh being returned
unopposed in 1952 for a second and final seven-year term—
and two referenda on the electoral system. Mr de Valera's can-
didature for the presidency in 1959 was deliberately linked
with a Fianna Fáil-sponsored attempt to replace proportional
representation by the straight vote. The PR referendum was
held on the same day (17 June 1959) as the presidential election,
and the double campaign slogan was 'Vote Yes and de Valera'.
But the majority of electors were not taken in by this transparent
political stratagem and made a nice distinction on polling day,
voting to retain proportional representation by 51.8 per cent
to 48.2 per cent while choosing de Valera as president by a
comfortable 12 per cent over his opponent, Seán MacEoin, prominent Fine Gael politician and veteran hero of the revolutionary
period.

When President de Valera stood for a second term in 1966,

his winning margin was considerably, not to say humiliatingly, narrower—a mere 10,000 votes in a poll of one million. The result, though all the more surprising in an anniversary year which recalled his role as 1916 commandant, was no reflection on his unique stature or on the distinction with which he had graced (and would continue to grace) the highest office in the land, but was rather due to the surprisingly effective campaign mounted by Fine Gael on behalf of T. F. O'Higgins whose theme was the need to humanise and rejuvenate the presidency. This diminution of Fianna Fáil prestige was followed in 1968 by a resounding popular rejection of the second attempt in a decade to get rid of proportional representation. The motive in 1959 had been a mixture of genuine concern to stabilise the political system and fear of what the future might hold without de Valera. But on 16 October 1968 an impressive majority of voters (60.8 per cent), including a considerable section of party followers, regarded the latest move as an arrogant bid to copperfasten Fianna Fáil in power, and gave their verdict accordingly.

One exciting election begins this survey, and another completes it. In 1969, Labour carried the high hopes which had inspired Clann na Poblachta twenty-one years before. But we may point out, first of all, that it was now a much changed and simplified political scene. Representatives of six parties, as well as twelve independents, had been returned in the 1948 election. After 1969, there remained only the three large parties and a solitary independent. Since the 1950s, turbulent issues and charismatic personalities had tended to fade from Irish politics, and with them disappeared the smaller parties. Farming and other sectional interests had been absorbed into the major parties, and the streamlining of modern politics, with its highly expensive publicity techniques, had decimated the once numerous and colourful body of independents.

Two other features of the changing political scene should be noted. First, the level of education of politicians in general was now very much higher.[14] Secondly, deputies were more than ever expected by their electors to service their constituencies and live, or be based, in them. The heroes of the revolution had been largely exempt from such mundane obligations but, with their passing, localism strongly asserted itself.[15]

The star of the 1969 election was Jack Lynch who conducted an American presidential-type campaign. He had already four by-elections to his credit but the general election, against all the predictions, was a resounding personal victory, not only over the opponents of Fianna Fáil but over his own ambitious lieutenants, some of whom had condescendingly regarded him as a mere caretaker.

The 1969 campaign had other attractions for the sporting political public. Intellectuals, for the first time, left the groves of Irish academe to try their luck at the hustings. Individually, they performed quite well, aided by the glamorous publicity of television. But the socialist cause to which most of them pledged allegiance was roundly defeated. In 1948, Clann na Poblachta's attitudes to partition and to the repatriation of sterling assets—as inexpertly expounded from Clann platforms—were quickly seized on by the party's opponents to discredit it in the eyes of the electorate as immature and irresponsible, and Communistic to boot! There was a strikingly similar pattern in 1969. Some Labour speakers were inept in the exposition of the new socialist policies. For example, it was not always made clear that 'national-isation' meant community control of land for building purposes: the concept sometimes disastrously emerged as land national-isation *pur sang*. Nor did Labour's opponents scorn to use the still highly profitable red smear. As for clerical intervention, it was a minor and random factor, but the occasional anti-socialist sermons *were* preached.

But this made little difference to the outcome. The new evangel was rejected by the men of great and small and no property. As our period ends, Labour was no better off than in 1922. True, it had grown significantly in the Dublin area but was un-represented in Connaught, the three Ulster counties and in the cities of Cork, Waterford and Galway. After June 1969, Fianna Fáil appeared permanently destined for power. Goliath, it seemed, was invincible. David had come to terms with the bitter reality that the New Republic was stillborn and the 1970s would not be Socialist, after all.

NOTES

1. John A. Murphy, 'The Irish Party System, 1938–51', *Ireland in the War Years and After*, Dublin 1969, 158–162.
2. Clann na Poblachta election poster, reproduced in M. E. Collins, *Ireland Three*, Dublin 1972, 239.
3. See the section on Clann na Poblachta in Maurice Manning, *Irish Political Parties*, Dublin 1972, 101–106. This most useful handbook supplies concise information on parties and elections up to 1969.
4. For a detailed study of Fine Gael's fluctuating fortunes, see John D. Walsh, 'The Decline and Resurgence of Fine Gael, 1938–54', unpublished M.A. thesis, UCC, 1978.
5. Brian Farrell, *Chairman or Chief? The Role of Taoiseach in Irish Government*, Dublin 1971.
6. Cf. his unequivocal statement in 1953, 'I am an Irishman second; I am a Catholic first . . . If the Hierarchy gives me any direction with regard to Catholic social teaching or Catholic moral teaching, I accept without qualification in all respects the teaching of the Hierarchy and the Church to which I belong.' Dáil Éireann, *Parliamentary Debates*, vol. 138, col. 840, 29 April 1953.
7. See A. S. Cohan, *The Irish Political Elite*, Dublin 1972.
8. Quoted in Farrell, *Chairman or Chief?*, 61.
9. Cf. Brendan Corish, *The New Republic*, Dublin 1968.
10. Manning, *Irish Political Parties*, 59–60, 114–18.
11. Cf. Conor Brady, 'The Party : an analysis of Fianna Fáil', *The Irish Times*, 19 July 1978.
12. E.g. Backbencher (John Healy) in *The Irish Times* on Saturdays.
13. David Thornley, 'Television and Politics', *Administration*, XV, 3, Autumn 1967, 217–25; Basil Chubb, *The Government and Politics of Ireland*, Stanford and London 1970, 142, 153–56. The Lemass statement was made in Dáil Éireann, *Parliamentary Debates*, vol. 224, col. 1046, 12 October 1966.
14. Brian Farrell, 'Irish Government Re-Observed', *Economic and Social Review*, VI, 3, April 1975, 411.
15. Tom Garvin, 'Continuity and Change in Irish Electoral Politics, 1923–69', *Economic and Social Review*, III, 3 April 1972, particularly 360–63.

BIBLIOGRAPHY

Some of the notes provide an obvious guide to further reading, and the sources there cited are not repeated in the following.

Newspaper coverage

(a) General elections: January-February, 1948; May-June, 1951; April-May, 1954; February-March, 1957; September-October, 1961; March-April, 1965; May-June, 1969.

(b) Referenda: May-June, 1959; September-October, 1968.

Election Results and Transfer of Votes (Stationery Office, Dublin): official returns for all elections since 1948.

Busteed, M. A. and Mason, H., 'Irish Labour in the 1969 Election', *Political Studies*, XVIII, 3, September 1970.

Chubb, Basil, 'Ireland, 1957' in D. E. Butler (ed.), *Elections Abroad*, London 1959.

Chubb, Basil, 'The Republic of Ireland' in S. Henig and J. Pindar (eds), *European Political Parties*, London 1969.

Farrell, Brian, 'Dail Deputies: "The 1969 Generation" ', *Economic and Social Review*, II, 3, April 1971.

O'Leary, Cornelius, *Irish Elections 1918–77: parties, voters and proportional representation*, Dublin 1979. Discusses the origin and development of the Irish variant of PR, its effect on party fortunes in elections, and the referendum campaign of 1959.

O'Leary, Cornelius, 'Under the Microscope: Election '65', *Irish Independent*, 21 April, 1965.

Viney, M. and Dudley Edwards, O., 'Parties and Power' in Dudley Edwards, O. (ed.), *Conor Cruise O'Brien Introduces Ireland*, London 1969.

Whyte, John, *Dáil Deputies* (Tuairim Pamphlet No. 15, Dublin 1966).

Whyte, John, 'Ireland' in Rd. Rose (ed.), *Electoral Behaviour: A Comparative Handbook*, London 1974.

Newspaper supplements to mark fiftieth anniversary of founding of Fianna Fáil: *The Irish Times*, 19 May, 1976; *The Irish Press*, 26 May, 1976.

General background

Lyons, F. S. L., *Ireland since the Famine*, London 1971.

Murphy, John A., *Ireland in the Twentieth Century*, Dublin 1975.

Sean Lemass

J. J. Lee

Sean Lemass finally succeeded Mr de Valera as Taoiseach in 1959. He had been the main architect of industrialisation in southern Ireland since he first became Minister of Industry and Commerce in 1932. But he had lacked the opportunity to stamp his style on Irish society, or even on economic policy as a whole, until de Valera retired. The Department of Finance, in particular, had fought a skilful delaying action to frustrate many of the initiatives emanating from Industry and Commerce during his long tenure as Minister.[1]

Lemass, who was already sixty, entered on a difficult political inheritance. It is one of the most thankless tasks in politics, as Anthony Eden and Ludwig Erhard could testify, to succeed a charismatic chief to whom one has long played second fiddle. The interminable wait can sap the energy, warp the judgment and corrode the idealism of all but the strongest personalities. Had Lemass become leader of Fianna Fáil between 1948 and 1957 he would have inherited a party which had lost much of its romantic aura of invincibility, and which would have been grateful for relatively meagre electoral success. But Fianna Fáil won a handsome majority in the General Election of 1957. That majority was quite deceptive. It was won on the lowest turnout since 1944. It amounted less to a vote of confidence in Fianna Fáil than to a vote of no confidence in the inter-party government held responsible for the worst economic crisis since the founding of the state. That economic crisis had not yet been decisively solved by 1959. It is true that T. K. Whitaker's *Economic Development*, and the *White Paper on Economic Expansion* in November 1958 roused enthusiasm among informed observers. But much of the more vulgar public response remained defeatist. The *Irish Independent*, admittedly associated with the opposition, attempted to place the *White Paper* in perspective with the perceptive headline 'Easier Credit Schemes for Farmers Proposed'.[2] The *Independent* waited three days before deciding to find space for a leading article on the *White Paper*, which it characteristically criticised for trying 'to do too much at once'.[3] If slightly later observers in 1958 felt that 'a new spirit, very different from the dejection of 1956 and most of 1957, motivated the actors'[4] emigration and unemployment nonetheless remained high throughout 1959 and 1960. The promise of the *White Paper* could not be translated into instant performance. It was therefore virtually inevitable that Fianna Fáil would lose support at the next election. Lemass would naturally be blamed for failing to fill de Valera's shoes. Some felt that Fianna Fáil's electoral fortunes were so dependent on de Valera that no successor could hope to maintain the party's hold on the electorate.[5]

In the event, Fianna Fáil did lose heavily in the 1961 election, with a low turnout still reflecting uncertain public morale. Lemass had to lead a minority government until the next election in 1965. It tells something of his political skill—and nerve— that this minority government has come to be widely regarded as among the best, if not the best, the state has ever enjoyed. It is true that if Fianna Fáil's majority between 1957 and 1961 was deceptive, the minority between 1961 and 1965 was also deceptive. Once it became clear early in the tenure of the new government that a turning point had been reached in the history of the state, that the Irish were indeed capable of self-government, the pall of gloom that enveloped the 1950s began to lift, and Lemass began to reap the rewards. The fear of another general election, which was now expected to strengthen Fianna Fáil, deterred independent deputies from voting against the government on crucial divisions in 1963, while by-election victories in Cork City and Kildare in early 1964 revealed the underlying strength of the government's position. The result of the 1965 general election was nonetheless remarkable. De Valera had on three occasions—in 1933, in 1938 and in 1944—increased his support in successive elections, but on each occasion thanks only to some spectacular stroke of policy or to bitter splits in the opposition. On every previous occasion on which Fianna Fáil went to the country after more than a year in office—not only in 1961, but in 1937, 1943, 1948, and 1954—it lost votes. 1965 was the first election in which Fianna Fáil—or indeed any government—increased its vote after a normal four and a half years in office. Turnout increased by nearly five per cent. Previous increases of this magnitude had brought sharp losses in votes to Fianna Fáil ever since 1933. Now it brought gains. The Fianna Fáil share of the vote rose from 43.8 to 47.7 per cent, its highest proportion since 1938, and its number of seats increased from seventy to seventy-two, sufficient to give an overall majority.

Lemass therefore laid the electoral ghost of de Valera in the general election of 1965, one of the least spectacular, and one of the most significant, in the annals of the state. But his place in Irish history depends much less on his ability to achieve power than on his ability to use it. He strongly supported Mr Whitaker, the gifted new secretary of the Department of Finance, in emphasising the necessity for rational economic and social planning. He also grasped more quickly than most the wider implications of the planning revolution. He appreciated, for instance, that planning required a transformation in civil service attitudes, the fostering of new mentalities and, in a sense, of new moralities. He criticised the civil service tendency 'to wait for new ideas to walk in through the door'.[6] This attitude was subversive of much venerable civil service doctrine, as indeed it remains in some quarters to this day. The immediate reaction of some civil servants was to jerk themselves sufficiently to get up to shut and bolt the door. Lemass even floated the heretical idea that civil service departments should view themselves as development corporations, and actually encourage initiative. He strongly supported the Development Division of the Department of Finance, established in 1959 shortly after he became Taoiseach, which was to play an important part in sustaining the economic recovery, and whose very title symbolised the changing concepts of the role of the civil service held by at least a few senior public servants.

The acceptance of planning initiated significant changes in the decision-making processes, and therefore ultimately in the power structure, of Irish society. The First Programme for Economic Expansion in 1958 achieved its immediate objective of dispelling defeatist gloom about the economic future of the country. But that was a once-for-all achievement. The problem of the early 1960s was how to sustain the recovery. The importance of this issue can too easily be overlooked. There had been previous spurts of growth, however narrowly based, in the Irish economy. They had invariably been followed by stagnation or even decline. As recently as 1957 incipient recovery had appeared to set in early in the year, only to falter alarmingly once more in the final quarter. There was no guarantee that the convalescence that began in 1958 would not be followed by relapse. The Second Programme for Economic Expansion launched in 1964 was much more ambitious and detailed than the first. It soon ran into trouble. Neither employers nor trade unions, government departments nor state sponsored bodies behaved according to the Plan's optimistic assumptions. The government reaction was to embark on a major campaign of education through consultation. Already in 1963 the government established the National Industrial and Economic Council as an independent body, but under the chairmanship of Mr Whitaker, with a membership including leading representatives of employer and labour organisations, as well as senior civil servants and leading academic economists. The NIEC began an attempt to pull and drag other state institutions, as well as employers and trade unions, into accepting some sort of responsibility for the longer term implications of planning. It emphasised that state bodies should plan in the context of the overall national plan, instead of behaving as independent republics. It had reservations about the quality of leadership in employer organisations and in trade unions, and urged that these bodies should haul themselves into the twentieth century. It berated employers and workers for trying to grab what they could of the fruits of planning, while shirking responsibility for failures. It emphasised that pressure groups had their duties as well as their rights. The ironic situation arose where civil servants who a decade before had been denouncing planning as weakminded, if not inherently evil, now found themselves urging private firms to imitate the state by trying to plan ahead for a few years. In 1965 the NIEC levelled at private enterprise the same sort of criticism that Lemass had levelled at the civil service : 'At present, too few firms plan positively for expansion; too many are passive, reacting tardily to increases in demand for their products.'[7]

Planning by consent required the support of workers on factory and shop floors. The NIEC therefore insisted that good communications were essential within trade unions, between officials and workers, between trade unionists and employers, and between the government and all of these bodies. It urged employers to plan ahead in consultation with their workers' representatives. All these developments arose in the short-term from the necessity to plan intelligently. Not all the suggestions were, of course, implemented immediately. Some would remain pious hopes well into the future. By no means all employers and workers, in the public or the private sectors, were grateful for unsolicited exhortation. Taken together, however, the stream of suggestions and recommendations began a subtle shift in the nature of public decision-making. They began the integration of management and trade unions into the formulation of public policy, institutionalised partly through the National Employer/Labour Conference, which made the two sides of industry to some extent 'social partners' with the government in decision-making rather than exclusively private interests. The successive economic plans involved increasing consultation with these 'partners'. The government accepted that the main economic power groups in society were entitled to their say in national planning—but these groups should themselves be rationally organised. The NIEC urged 'a joint body for each industry representing management and workers' because this 'would obviate the problems that now arise because of the existence of a multiplicity of bodies'. More intelligent employers and trade unionists began to appreciate, as they consulted with top-class civil servants and economists on the NIEC, and on the various councils and committees that were established to improve industrial productivity, that they had to streamline their own organisations and improve the quality of their services, or else they would find themselves out of their depth in a changing economic environment. Partly as a result of this, and despite much dogged resistance, the quality of leadership in the employers' organisations including the agricultural organisations, and in the trade unions, improved significantly during the 1960s.

Lemass thus presided over the establishment of new procedures for economic and social decision-making. Under his aegis, Ireland began to shuffle towards a version of the corporate state. Cor-

poratism, understood in the general sense in which it was pro-
pounded by Pope Pius XI in his encyclical *Quadragesimo Anno*
in 1931, had become rather fashionable in some circles in the
1930s. It was, in principle, an attempt to avoid the extremes of
either capitalism or communism—of undiluted private greed on
the one hand, or of totalitarian central control on the other—
by the creation of self-governing corporations, consisting of representatives of all the interests in particular industries and pro-
fessions, which would protect their members against exploitation
either by individuals or by the state. The government appointed
a Commission on Vocational Organisation in 1939, which submitted an ambitious report in 1943.[8] A bitter critic of that report
was none other than Sean Lemass, who engaged in a wrangle,
as undignified as it was unworthy, with the chairman, Michael
Browne, Bishop of Galway.

The apparent inconsistency, however, between Lemass's
attitude in the 1940s and in the 1960s was to some extent super-
ficial. He had lamented throughout his career that the various
private interests in Irish society were badly organised and poorly
represented. He found it exasperating to have to negotiate with
individual firms and to discuss isolated proposals, often presented
by incompetents who had not done their homework properly—
they wasted his time. He considered it more rational to negotiate
with organisations which could represent their members effectively. His idea of corporatism differed in one basic respect from
that of the Commission on Vocational Organisation. The Commission regarded vocational bodies as alternatives to the civil
service; it criticised civil servants for doing too much. Lemass
criticised them for doing too little. The Commission wanted a
corporate society, Lemass a corporate state. The Commission
criticised the civil service for failing to consult adequately with
interested parties. In the 1960s, the government was trying to
find interested parties worth consulting. Lemass's corporate state
embraced the civil service and private enterprise as partners in a
common adventure, not as mutually exclusive sources of decision-
making, and Lemass himself drew his inspiration less from papal
pronouncements than from the planning techniques developed
particularly in France and Italy after the Second World War.

The new corporatism—Lemass did not of course call it that
—diminished even further the authority of the Dáil. The Dáil

had never counted for much in effective decision-making in economic and social policy. But this had been disguised when most economic policy decisions were negative ones to do nothing, rather than positive ones to do something. The essential planning decisions were now taken outside parliament, just as the essential non-planning decisions had previously been taken outside parliament. It seems clear that Lemass himself had little confidence in the capacity of the average Dáil member to contribute intelligently to economic decision-making.[9]

Lemass's corporatism was functional rather than ideological. The western world was moving in that general direction in any event, and Lemass's function was to give more coherent shape and more decisive momentum to the development in Ireland. But there was an ideology lurking beneath the fabled pragmatism. When Lemass proclaimed that 'the historic task of this generation is to secure the economic foundation of independence'[10] he not only cast cold reflection on the achievement of previous governments—not excluding those in which he himself had served—but he threw a time bomb into Irish history, attempting to divert the mainstream, and to launch the rising generation on a momentous mission, which promised at long last to banish to the rubbish dump of history the wailing of Caitlín Ni hUalachain, the champion whiner of the western world, the princess of the begging bowl, and to create a viable Irish society, self-confident without being unduly self-righteous. For a man commonly dismissed as a mere pragmatist this was an almost ludicrously idealistic ambition, amounting to nothing less than an attempt to transform a people's self-image and even their very character. Sean McEntee was to describe him as 'by temperament and by predilection . . . a merchant adventurer'.[11] There were few societies in Europe which appeared to offer less scope to a merchant adventurer than the stagnant Ireland of the mid-twentieth century. Only a conquistador of the spirit, however pragmatic his short-term tactics, could have embarked on such a venture.

Lemass also felt that this was the only way that Ulster Protestants could be enticed into a united Ireland.[12] They must be attracted, not coerced. How Ulster unionists could be expected to want to join a state from which thousands of its own citizens were fleeing mystified him. He considered Ulster

Protestant traditions to be as genuine and valuable as Irish Catholic ones. He emphasised the positive values of Ulster protestantism, and rejected the cultural imperialism of Irish Irelanders or Catholic Irelanders. He thought it would be disastrous for Ireland if the south could end partition by force because it would then set up a police state in the north.[13] The conviction that partition 'is entirely a mental attitude' and that 'unity has got to be thought of as a spiritual development which will be brought about by peaceful, persuasive means'[14] inspired his meetings with Terence O'Neill, which marked the first significant breach in the wall of official suspicion between north and south. Lemass may have been wrong and his hopes may have been hopelessly illusory. But his way cannot be claimed to have failed as it has never been seriously tried. His basic generosity of spirit was closer to the tradition of Tone than were many who would denounce his pragmatism in the name of their bastard republicanism.

Lemass never wavered in his ultimate ideal of a free, united, and prosperous Ireland. What distinguished him from other idealists, and has earned the reputation for pragmatism, was that he actually set out to achieve his ideal instead of simply proclaiming it. Politics was a means to an end, not an end in itself. Incantation was no substitute for intelligence. This led him to place particular importance on the role of the individual in Irish society, but the growth of society was in turn a pre-requisite for the development of the individual. A stunted society meant stunted personalities. Without expansion, as C. F. Andrews was to put it, 'there is no hope . . . beyond waiting for the other fellow to die'.[15] Lemass was concerned with the human problems of organisation, with sustaining motivation in the face of frequent discouragement, whose dangers he had more reason than most to appreciate. He knew that the main obstacle to economic development—and to all the creativity dependent on that development—was the mediocrity of so many decision-makers. He scarcely bothered to conceal his contempt for the calibre of many businessmen and trade unionists. 'The industrial forest must be cleared of deadwood' he urged in 1959 and went some distance towards clearing the political forest of its deadwood setting out to emphasise his priorities by encouraging talent, by rewarding merit, by fostering a public morality by which achievement would be recognised and, if possible, lack of achievement penalised. 'Young men are coming along in the party now and their mind is set on when they will reach the stage of being in line for consideration for a ministerial appointment. They will feel frustrated if they see men remaining in office whom they feel are less competent than themselves or so old that they should be retired. I . . . would have kept on making changes time and again—if for no other reason than to make it quite clear to any new man that if he showed he had ability the road to promotion was fairly open to him.'[16] Only thus could a viable society be created in Ireland which would vindicate the achievement of political independence by offering Irish people a decent chance to earn the reward for ability long denied to them, a decent chance of keeping their family in Ireland, and a decent chance to educate their children. Lemass was the first Taoiseach to take education seriously. He appointed some of his ablest ministers, P. J. Hillery, George Colley, and finally the rumbustious Donogh O'Malley, to the Department of Education. These promising young ministers had a future to carve out, and therefore an incentive to do something, in contrast to the previous type of minister associated with education. Time and again Lemass emphasised that the performance of state-sponsored bodies, civil service departments, industry and trade unions—he might have added all the other institutions, not least the universities—depended on the quality of the men at the helm. In a small society with no inherent momentum of its own and with a heritage of stagnation, it was men that mattered. The initiative, or lack of it, of a handful of individuals could make or mar important institutions for a generation.[17]

Irish society could not be cleared of most of its deadwood in the seven short years of his premiership. A people's psyche, the values ingrained in the older generations, their concepts of public morality, cannot be transformed at a stroke. Lemass set out on the first stage of a long hard slog to change mentalities ingrained over the centuries. He was confronted by that pervasive mediocrity which gave the Irish, after nearly forty years of independence, the lowest living standards, the highest emigration rates, the worst unemployment rates, and the most intellectually stultifying society in northern Europe. Lemass was well aware of the viscosity of Irish society, sucking down men of ability, energy and idealism to the level of the limpets clinging to their pension rights. Success would come only after a long grinding siege, if it came at all. His achievement cannot be measured by what he accomplished in his own short premiership. The test was whether his work would survive him, whether the momentum he generated would continue. In this sense he was in large measure successful. De Valera lingered beyond his age and the legacy of Lemass lived after him. Despite all the discouragements and setbacks, and there would be many, despite the clinging survivals of earlier mentalities, Lemass succeeded in establishing a bridgehead in which the productive forces in Irish society could take root, and gradually—however gradually—push back the parasitic forces.

Lemass rose splendidly to the daunting challenge of succeeding de Valera, the giant of an earlier epoch. And he practiced what he preached. He himself resigned in 1966, at the relatively early age of 67. His health had deteriorated but he still had the energy and drive of many men in their prime. But it was in accordance with his own principles to move over when he felt he had given of his best. 'It is time I moved on. I don't want to become a national monument around the place.' There was a rough honesty about Lemass that more scrupulous public moralists rarely managed to emulate. It was natural that he should believe in the career open to talents. He was the first man to become Taoiseach simply because he stood head and shoulders above his rivals in terms of sheer ability. W. T. Cosgrave had become President of the Executive Council in 1922 through his relative seniority following in the steps of Collins and Griffith. De Valera owed his initial eminence to the chance of survival in 1916. John A. Costello became Taoiseach because he was not Richard Mulcahy. All three achieved their position initially through short-term accident. Lemass reached his through long-term achievement. This naturally moulded his outlook and reinforced his conviction that a close relationship should exist between merit and reward. However loose that relationship remains in Irish society, it was far closer after Lemass than before him. Meritocracy of course exacts its own price. There are values that cannot be encompassed within a narrow version of it. But there are even more values, not least intellectual and cultural values, which cannot begin to be satisfied without

B

it. 'A mould breaker and a mould maker', the *Irish Times* was to rightly call Lemass in a perceptive obituary appraisal.[18] Rare indeed are the public figures of whom it could be seriously suggested, as the *Times* went on to suggest of Lemass, that 'he came to power too late—he left power too early'.[19]

NOTES

1. This emerges clearly from Ronan Fanning, *The Irish Department of Finance, 1922–58*, Dublin 1978.
2. *Irish Independent*, Nov. 12, 1958.
3. *Ibid.*, Nov. 15, 1958.
4. *Irish Review and Annual*, 1958, 11.
5. See, for instance, Political Correspondent, *Irish Times*, Nov. 22, 1958, 1.
6. S. F. Lemass, 'The Organization behind the Economic Programme', *Administration*, IX, 1, 1961, reprinted in B. Chubb & P. Lynch, *Economic Development and Planning*, Dublin 1969, 205.
7. NIEC, Report no. 8, 1965, reprinted in Chubb & Lynch, *op. cit.*, 274-90.
8. For an analysis of some features of Irish corporatist thinking see Joseph Lee, 'Some aspects of Corporatist thought in Ireland : the Commission on Vocational Organization, 1939–43', in A. Cosgrove, (ed.), *Studies in Irish History, presented to R. D. Edwards*, Naas 1979.
9. See, for instance, the reservations he expresses discreetly in 'The role of the state sponsored bodies', *Administration*, VI, 4, 1959, reprinted in Chubb & Lynch, *op. cit.*, 191.
10. Dail Debates, 175, Col. 938, June 3, 1959.
11. *Irish Press*, May 12, 1971.
12. 'Sean Lemass looks back', 8, *Irish Press*, January 28, 1969.
13. *Ibid.*
14. *Ibid.*
15. Chubb and Lynch, *op. cit.*, 195.
16. B. Farrell, *Chairman or Chief?*, Dublin 1971, 61. This whole chapter (55–73) provides a discerning appraisal of Lemass.
17. See, for example, his emphasis that 'the performance of a State corporation depends, in our experience, on the capacities of the individual holding the chief executive post . . .', Chubb and Lynch, *op. cit.*, 189.
18. *Irish Times*, May 12, 1971.
19. *Ibid.*

Economic Growth and Development, 1945-70

Brendan M. Walsh

After the stagnation of the Great Depression and the austerity of the war years, Ireland experienced an economic boom during the immediate post-war period. The volume of personal spending rose by about one quarter between 1946 and 1950. It was natural that a consumer spree should occur as the purchasing power that had been pent up during the war was released. But growth also occurred in the level of exports, as Irish industry took advantage of the expansion of overseas markets, and tourism benefited from the shortages of food and foreign exchange in Britain. With some help from Marshall Aid, a Public Capital Programme was introduced and considerable sums were allocated for schools, hospitals and housing, as well as roads, airports, and harbours.

The Census of 1951 recorded an increase of five thousand over the population of 1946. Although this increase was slight, and confined entirely to Dublin and five other Leinster counties, it brought to an end over a century of national population decline and provided grounds for the belief that an era of moderate growth was dawning.

The 1950s were not very old, however, before the grounds for optimism were swept away. Adverse external developments compounded by inappropriate policy responses quickly halted the economic growth of the immediate post-war years. To understand the sequence of events that led to economic stagnation during the 1950s we must bear in mind the importance of the balance of payments in the mind of economic policy makers both in Ireland and abroad during this period. If domestic demand was allowed to expand too rapidly, according to the prevailing view, resources would be diverted from export markets, imports would be drawn into the country at an accelerating pace, and the balance of payments deficit would rise to an alarming level. This deficit would have to be paid for by running down our external reserves—a process which could not continue indefinitely. Sooner or later the authorities would be forced to take 'corrective' action by deflating the domestic economy through higher taxation and severe economies in the public sector, or by curbing the level of imports more directly through special taxes or levies. Balance would be restored at a lower level of domestic economic activity. The possibility that the payments deficit would set in train deflationary forces, and thus prove largely self-correcting, was not seriously entertained by orthodox economic opinion in Europe or America at this time.

Twice during the 1950s, in 1952 and 1956, the authorities responded in this manner to what were perceived as balance of payments crises. The Budget of 1952 halted the upward trend in public capital spending that was apparent since 1946. The drastic cut-backs following the 1955 crisis actually reduced the volume of government spending by 15 per cent between 1956 and 1958. This led to a fall in the public sector's share in national income from 35 to 30 per cent. There was however only a slight fall in the level of public sector employment. The brunt of the economies fell on the level of employment in the private sector, as public spending on housing, roads and related activity was sharply reduced. The level of employment in the building and construction sector fell from 74,000 in 1955 to 56,000 in 1958. The numbers out of work in Ireland rose to a peak of 78,000 in 1957, but in an era where Unemployment Benefits were low and expired after six months, leaving the unemployed dependant on Assistance, it is not surprising that the full extent of the recession was reflected in the emigration, rather than in the unemployment figures. At this time, the unemployment rate was very low in Britain and jobs were readily available to Irish migrants. The numbers leaving the country soared to a level that had not been seen since the troubled decade of the 1880s. In the worst year, 1957, the net loss of population due to emigration reached 54,000, while between 1951 and 1961 it totalled over 400,000. The slight gain of population between 1946 and 1951 was erased, and by 1961 the population had declined to 2.8 million, more than 5 per cent below the level at the foundation of the state. This was a bitter outcome indeed to those who believed, with Padraig Pearse, that in a free Ireland the population would rapidly expand and eventually surpass the pre-Famine total.

The feeling of demoralisation and failure generated by this situation is conveyed in a paragragh of the report *Economic Development* submitted by the Secretary of the Department of Finance to the Government in 1958:

> After 35 years of native government people are asking whether we can achieve an acceptable degree of economic progress. The common talk among parents in the towns, as well as in rural Ireland, is of their children having to emigrate as soon as their education is completed in order to secure a reasonable standard of living.

The balance of payments crises which provoked the restrictive measures were largely a reflection of the impact of external events on the Irish economy rather than a consequence of domestic profligacy. The 1950 crisis was caused by a sudden rise in import prices following the devaluation of the pound sterling from $4.00 to $2.80 in September 1949 and the jump in raw material prices following the outbreak of war in Korea in the summer of 1950. The deterioration in the balance of payments following the surge in import prices would have been temporary and self-correcting, and in fact had largely corrected itself by the time the deflationary measures contained in the 1952 Budget began to take effect. In 1955, while it is true that a domestic consumer boom contributed to a rapid growth of imports, the real problem lay in a slump in our cattle trade to Britain and our displacement from the British egg market. The deficit incurred in 1955 was not much more than half that incurred in 1951 but for the first time since the war, the net inflow of capital to the country was turned into an outflow in 1955. This reflected the slowing-down in economic growth, the loss of confidence in the economy, and drying up of profitable outlets for capital in Ireland. The decline of nearly one quarter in Ireland's external reserves during 1955 was the signal to which the authorities responded, and the measures taken in 1956 were designed to restore balance to external trade, to reverse the decline in external reserves, and place the economy on a sounder and more creditworthy basis.

It is easy to criticise these policy responses with hindsight.

However, there were a number of obstacles to better decision-making, such as delays in data availability, and unfamiliarity with the need to adjust quarterly series for seasonality. Moreover, the degree of sophistication in Irish policy-making could not with impunity outpace that of the international banking community, which still viewed an independent Irish economy as a dubious proposition. These considerations would have made it very hard to follow the presumptions of some contemporary theorists who view the balance of payments as essentially self-regulating if treated with benign neglect by the authorities. Nonetheless it is fair to say that a narrow view was taken of the role of foreign reserves and of the need to restore external balance by government action rather than through market forces. Moreover, delays in diagnosing and responding to the problem led to the situation both in 1952 and 1956 that by the time the corrective measures began to take effect there were clear signs that the worst was over. Undoubtedly the effect of the massive cut-backs in government spending in 1956 and subsequent years was to prolong the recession and make its impact more severe than would have been the case if the level of spending had followed longer term guidelines and shown less erratic year-to-year swings. Although the ratio of foreign reserves to imports declined substantially during the 1950s, this ratio remained high by international standards. The ultimate justification for holding such reserves is to tide a country over exceptionally adverse periods such as we can now recognise 1955 to have been. However, it was not until 1969 that the Government negotiated with the country's commercial banks the placing on deposit with the Central Bank of their net external assets. Failure to mobilise reserves during the 1950s in order to maintain output and unemployment undoubtedly led to unnecessary sacrifices borne mainly by the unemployed and the emigrants.

The disappointing economic performance of the years 1953 to 1958, which saw no growth in GNP and a decline in population, provoked a great deal of self-criticism and revaluation among those responsible for advising the government on the overall direction of economic policy. The fruits of this reappraisal were published in the Department of Finance's study of national development problems, *Economic Development*, from which we quoted above. Although largely ignored by the

Press at the time of publication, this document is now generally recognised to have played a key role in redirecting government thinking and in preparing the way for the new economic policies of the 1960s. A major theme of this report was the support it gave to the view long advocated by the Central Bank that 'public and private development of a productive character must be stimulated and organised so as to overshadow the non-productive development which now bulks so largely in public investment . . .'. Funds were to be directed into state aid to marketing and research, land improvements, the development of new industries, fishery, and tourism. To facilitate a higher level of expenditure on these 'productive' projects, it was hoped to raise the volume of current savings. But the main source of funds for the new departures in government spending was to be a cut-back in the level of social or 'non-productive' spending, that is, in the public housing programme, the capital outlay for the health services and generally by deferring further improvements in the social services until economic recovery was well underway.

The publication of this study was by way of letting the public in on the detailed discussions that had led to the policies adopted in the White Paper published slightly earlier in 1958. This document ushered in an era of official commitment to some form of economic planning which lasted until 1972. The First Programme covered the years 1959 to 1963 and devoted considerable attention to the failures of past policies in much the same language as appeared in the Department of Finance's economic study. The word 'plan' was avoided, no hard and fast numerical targets were proposed, and the emphasis was on an approach and a policy bias rather than on detailed intervention with a predominantly free enterprise economy.

One area where a new departure occurred was in the attitude towards international trade and investment. During the 1930s, in an international environment of protectionism and autarky, an elaborate system of tariffs and quotas had been erected to stimulate native industrial development. Foreign ownership of industrial assets was discouraged. The emphasis was on development of native resources through native skills and enterprise. As the 1950s progressed Ireland's commitment to these policies of economic isolationism was considerably modified. As part of the revaluation of economic policy following the poor performance of the early 1950s, the movement towards an outward-looking strategy became more rapid. The implications of the ground-swell of Free Trade in Europe for the sheltered Irish industrial sector were recognised. In 1961 the government appointed a Committee on Industrial Organisation to 'make a critical appraisal of the measures that might have to be taken to adopt Irish industry to conditions of more intensive competition in home and export markets.' The work of this Committee resulted in detailed studies of twenty-two industries, and is contained in its *Final Report* (Stationery Office 1965, Pr. 8082).

A new urgency was placed on attracting export-oriented industries as well as expanding traditional foreign exchange earners such as tourism. The powers and resources of the Industrial Development Authority were expanded progressively, and the restrictions on foreign investment in the Control of Manufactures Act relaxed and eventually removed. Shannon Duty Free Airport was transformed into a Development Company which established a unique growth centre west of the Shannon based entirely on manufacturing for export. In the ten years 1960–69 more than 350 new foreign-owned companies were established in Ireland. Without these it is unlikely that the rapid growth rate of industrial exports achieved in the 1950s would have been maintained during the 1960s: new foreign firms locating in Ireland during the 1960s averaged an export ratio over 80 per cent of output. The injection of new resources into the tourist industry and the development of new markets in North America and Europe resulted in an accelerated growth of foreign exchange earnings from this source. However, the various measures that were taken were far less successful in transforming traditional, home-market-oriented firms into dynamic, export-oriented enterprises, and in this failure lay the seeds of the persistently disappointing performance in terms of overall growth of employment. With the advent of full free trade in the 1970s, the loss of employment in many traditional and highly labour-intensive industries negated much of the employment growth in the new and more capital intensive sectors.

The formal end of the era of protectionism in Ireland was signalled by its first application for membership in the European Economic Community in 1961. Although actual entry into the community was still twelve years away, it was clear from the date of the first application that it was only a matter of time before free trade became a reality. Less dramatic but of much greater immediate significance than application for membership in the EEC was the signing of the Anglo-Irish Free Trade Agreement in December 1965. This Agreement brought to a close the attempt at economic development based on protectionism launched in the 1930s and returned Ireland to the close economic ties with the United Kingdom that had characterised the period 1800–1922. The important difference now lay in the determination of the Irish government to use its powers of taxation and expenditure to maximise the gains to the country from its participation in the world economy, and to obtain favourable treatment for its agricultural exports. In the event, Ireland's participation in this simple type of free trade area was short-lived because membership of the EEC became a reality in 1973. The European Community is not merely a Free Trade Area but is also committed to equalising differentials in living standards between regions of the Community through institutions such as the Common Agricultural Policy and the Regional and Social Funds. Moreover, Ireland's membership of the largest trading bloc in the world enormously increased the country's attractiveness as a location for foreign, and in particular American, investment.

During the period of the First Programme for Economic Expansion the volume of GNP rose by over 4 per cent a year, which was faster than any of the tentative projections put forward in 1958. The government launched a Second Programme in 1963 to cover the seven-year period 1964–1970. This was a far more detailed and elaborate exercise than the First Programme. Not only was a growth rate of over 4 per cent per annum accepted as a target for the economy, but detailed checks on the implications of this growth rate for agriculture, industry and services were undertaken.

The overall growth target specified in the plan was in fact reached and economic growth during the 1960s was faster and more sustained than in any previous period in Irish history. Not only did living standards rise by 50 per cent over the decade but by 1971 the population had grown by over 100,000 from the low point of 1961 to the highest level recorded since the foundation of the state. Moreover, although the Dublin region's share in the national total continued to increase after 1961, growth spread out to more and more regions of the eastern and southern half of the country. Only in the west and north-west did the age-old pattern of population decline persist.

Despite these achievements, the contribution of economic planning remained debatable. Even though the overall target of raising living standards by 50 per cent was attained it became increasingly clear as the decade progressed that the detailed, sectoral projections in the Second Programme were not reliable. In particular, the growth of imports outstripped the projections in the Programme, and this led to a balance of payments crisis in 1966. Fortunately, this set-back was less severe, and the authorities' response to it less draconian, than was the case ten years earlier. More serious was the Programme's overestimation of the contribution of agriculture to national growth. Instead of an annual average expansion of almost 4 per cent, the volume of agricultural output in fact grew by less than one per cent. While much of this shortfall could be blamed on the delay in Ireland's accession to the EEC, it provided an important illustration of the way in which a Programme could incorporate targets without specifying the means for their achievement. As Desmond Norton pointed out in 1975, economic planning in Ireland tended to concentrate on the choice of targets and their implications for sectoral growth whereas economists prefer to think of planning as a process whereby policy instruments are selected and set at levels that will result in certain targets being reached. It has also been pointed out that a crude comparison of a programme's target with actual outcomes is not an adequate framework for planning evaluation. There is a need to evaluate how specific policies contributed to the performance of the economy over the period of the Plan and to try to identify how much of the observed performance of the economy can be attributed to the implementation of the programme. An exercise of this nature was not undertaken on the Irish programmes and the only evaluation that was envisioned by the planners was to be undertaken by the body responsible for formulating the programme, namely, the Department of Finance. In its periodic reviews of progress under the programme, the Department stressed the lack of national commitment to the programme and 'actions both in the public and private sectors that were out of line with the programme's objectives' as factors leading to the non-attainment of targets. This rationalisation in turn points to the absence of detailed departmental budgetary implications and guidelines from the programme, which, as Olympios Katsiouni pointed out in 1978, was a fundamental weakness of indicative planning as that term was understood in Ireland.

Perhaps the most disturbing and persistent discrepancy between the goals set out in successive programmes and the actual performance of the economy lay in the area of employment. The Second Programme called for a net increase of 81,000 in the level of employment between 1963 and 1970. As the plan period progressed, it became clear that the numbers engaged in agriculture were declining faster than anticipated, while the growth of industrial and service employment was slower than hoped. More of this growth was being achieved by increased productivity, and less by increased employment, than had been anticipated. The result was a net decline of 18,000 in the level of employment, a short-fall of almost 100,000 over the level projected in the Programme. Moreover, despite the growth of non-agricultural employment, the rate of unemployment was substantially higher at the end of the decade than at the beginning.

In the Third Programme for Economic and Social Development, introduced in 1969, there was a new emphasis on policies to reach full employment. This was taken to mean an unemployment rate of less than 4 per cent and annual net emigration of about 12,000. In fact, by 1970 the return flow of former emigrants more than offset the outflow of young people, and Ireland became a net gainer from migration for the first time in recorded history. This meant that the population was growing somewhat faster than its natural growth rate, which at over one per cent annually was the highest in western Europe.

The Second Programme was meant to cover the period 1964–70, but was officially abandoned in 1967. The Third Programme was designed for the period 1969–72, but very little was heard of it after its publication. Neither the Programmes themselves nor their eventual abandonment was discussed in Dáil Eireann. The verdict of economists writing in the 1970s has tended to the view that the whole planning exercise was seriously flawed from a methodological point of view (see Norton, 1975, and Katsiouni, 1978). Yet despite this, among a wider public the view persists that the Programmes made an important contribution to moving the Irish economy, and indeed Irish society, forward from the stagnation of the 1950s to the expansion and development of the 1960s. Perhaps much of the impact was psychological, in that the Programmes testified to a government commitment to economic development, and helped to replace the old political issues with discussion about the best means of building up the Irish economy. Industrialists were forced to take account of the changing international environment and of the need to adapt and expand in order to survive. Civil servants, especially in the key policy-making departments, were imbued with a new sense of priorities by the politicians who realised with increasing acuteness that their survival was closely linked to the performance of the economy. But whatever the importance of these factors, the major trends in the Irish economy continued to reflect international forces, such as the opening of new opportunities through membership of the EEC, the favourable climate for industrial exports during the boom years that ended in 1974, the accelerating inflation in the UK economy to which Ireland was linked in a close economic and monetary union, and even the repercussions of rising unemployment in the UK on young Irish people's willingness to emigrate.

The challenge of coping with rapid growth in the population and providing jobs for all those seeking employment in Ireland was to become a major theme of the 1970s. At the end of the 1960s, after more than a century of heavy emigration, it was understandable that the growth of population was more a source of pride in recent achievements than a cause of anxiety about the future. The nation faced into the new era of full membership in the EEC with a new confidence in the industrial, commercial and agricultural future of the economy, despite the darkening clouds of unemployment and inflation on the horizon.

BIBLIOGRAPHY

Chubb, Basil and Lynch, Patrick, (eds) *Economic Development and Planning*, vol. 1 of *Readings in Irish Public Administration*,

The Institute of Public Administration, Dublin 1969.

Committee of Industrial Organisation, *Final Report*, The Stationery Office, Dublin, 1965. (Pr. 8082).

Department of Finance, *Economic Development*, The Stationery Office, Dublin, 1958. (Pr. 4803).

Katsiouni, Olympios, 'Planning in a Small Economy "the Republic of Ireland" ', paper read to the Statistical and Social Inquiry Society of Ireland, May 1978.

Kennedy, Kieran A. and Dowling, Brendan R., *Economic Growth in Ireland:The Experience since 1947*, Gill and Macmillan, Dublin 1975.

McAleese, Dermot, 'Outward-looking policies, manufactured exports, and economic growth : the Irish experience' in M. J. Artis and A. R. Nobay (eds), Proceedings of AUTE Conference 1977, Oxford, Blackwells, 1978.

Norton, Desmond, *Problems in Economic Planning and Policy Formation in Ireland 1958–1974*, The Economic and Social Research Institute, Broadsheet no. 12, Dublin 1975.

Programme for Economic Expansion, The Stationery Office, Dublin 1958, (Pr. 4796).

Second Programme for Economic Expansion, Parts I and II, The Stationery Office, Dublin 1963 and 1964, (Pr. 7239 and Pr. 7670).

Business and Labour in Irish Society, 1945-70

John L. Pratschke

The study of the roles of Business and Labour in society is particularly important; the outlook and philosophy of a society at large is encapsulated and summarised in concrete form by the ways in which Business and Labour are organised, and by the way in which they make contact with one another, and with the rest of society. Other expressions of a society's view of itself, in artistic or literary forms, may impinge directly on the lives of but a few citizens, but our near-universal familiarity with work, and with the organisation of work, makes the structure of the institutions of Business and Labour of particular significance to us all.

The development of economic society has long been dominated by the division of labour, the notion that society's total production and welfare are enhanced when each task is subdivided into specialised component tasks which can be performed more expeditiously by one person. Job specialisation is a fundamental characteristic of virtually all societies that are economically developed. In the Irish case, the implementation of this principle implies, for Business and Labour in particular that each person is highly dependent on others to buy what he produces, and to produce what he buys, or what he works with; that the specialist is held in high regard by the society; and that the interaction between people, in their capacities as workers and organisers of workers, takes place within the market framework.

When the Second World War was finally ended, the Irish people in common with peoples everywhere aspired to a life of some comfort after the deprivation and distress of the Emergency. The fact that many Irish people had worked during the war in the United Kingdom, and acquired there a first hand experience of the scale and specialisation of an industrialised society, probably added to the pent-up pressure for an improvement in living conditions.

Unfortunately, despite the increased capital expenditure of the post-war years, economic recovery seemed to pass Ireland by. The important decisions taken to constitute the IDA in 1950, and An Foras Tionscail and Córas Tráchtála in 1952, seemed to be fruitless. Between 1949 and 1956, real national income rose by only 8 per cent, while Western Europe generally managed 40 per cent.

Against this unhappy background, it is hardly surprising that neither Business nor Labour were showing many signs of creativity. There was, however, a sense of achievement at the setting up of the Labour Court in 1946. In an earlier Thomas Davis series, James Plunket spoke of the Court as a symbol of

> the victory of trade unionism in its fight for a respected and influential place in the social and economic life of modern Ireland. Here was the beginning of a new stage in Labour relations, with its machinery for direct negotiations and conciliation representing new privileges for trade unionism, but also putting on its shoulders new responsibilities.[1]

By and large, it seems that the trade unions used their power in the post-war years moderately, and were not unreasonable in their approach to demands for pay increases.[2] The conditions of their members were significantly improved. Their failures concerned structures, which reflects rather well the pragmatic, low-key views of many of the leaders of the time. Heavy unemployment and continuing emigration did not aid the growth of trade unionism; nor did the continuing rifts between Larkin and O'Brien, between the WUI and IT and GWU, between the Irish TUC and the Congress of Irish Unions. The continuing cleavages between segments of the Labour movement certainly did not create the climate for the rationalisation of trade unions nor for success in the recruitment of clerical and service workers. These were the failures of the late 1940s and early 1950s—the continued fragmentation of trade unionism instead of consolidation, the failure to widen the movement to embrace enough of the hitherto unorganised. The stamp of O'Brien rather than of Larkin seemed to be impressed on these post-war years. The unions were forced to concentrate their energies on preserving as far as they could the living standards of their members, and on their own numerical strength, rather than in giving wider expression to the cherished ideal of solidarity with all workers. If the stance of the Labour organisations was essentially defensive, and if it used its new role in the Labour Court with moderation, it is more difficult to characterise the situation of Business in general. What is clear is that the private sector had not succeeded in leading the growth of output and incomes that all wished for. The predominantly small, family-owned and managed firms which produced small quantities of a relatively wide number of product lines for a protected home market was very substantially investigated more recently by the Committee on Industrial Organisation. Its many reports show clearly that Irish business needed to change substantially to be competitive in modern conditions. Lack of management skills, lack of creativity, but above all the lack of progressional commitment to the task of enterprise growth, these are the negative qualities, the failures most often attributed to Irish Business.

It is significant that the breed of professional business managers became evident first in the state-sponsored bodies, rather than in the private sector of established industry and commerce. In many instances, these state and semi-state organisations, which had grown on an ad hoc basis to fill glaring voids in Irish enterprise, led the way in the utilisation of modern techniques of organisation and management. Their success is one of the wonders and contradictions of modern post-war Ireland.

By the middle 1950s, however, the picture had become one of unrelieved gloom. As that much-quoted public servant Dr T. K. Whitaker has observed more recently:

> For the first half of the nineteen fifties economic progress had been brought almost to a standstill . . . The mood of despondency was palpable.[3]

Now in retrospect it seems inevitable that successive governments should have fallen in those grim days, but also it seems inevitable that the air of blank resignation to economic inevitability should eventually fade. It was replaced by the desire to determine, in part at least on a conscious planned basis, the development of the Irish economy. The sequence of events whereby the idea of engineering the economy away from stagnation can be summarised briefly : it was proposed by the Capital Investment Advisory Committee,[4] the idea was acted upon by Dr Whitaker and his associates in the public service,[5] the scheme was accepted by the government and was presented to the public as the First Programme for Economic Expansion.[6] And economic growth followed it. Academic economists and historians continue to discuss the role which the First Programme played or did not play in the growth which accompanied it, but it is fair to say that the popular reaction was one of near adulation for the technical experts who had formulated the deus ex machina.

Business and Labour reacted strongly and positively to the leadership and pragmatic style of the new Lemass government. While the First Programme may have descended somewhat unexpectedly upon them both, their involvement in the Second and Third Programmes was much greater. Indeed, it is the nature of the Second and Third Programmes in particular which stimulated the two most decisive changes in the organisation of Business and Labour. Both became more professional and more technical in orientation.

On the Business front, the incentive schemes, tax reliefs and other aids attracted to Ireland many new firms from abroad, and for these, and the existing Irish firms, the style of management changed. The crucial hold—some might say the stranglehold—of family ties over Irish industry and commerce was weakened. In its place came the new professional manager and administrator. Financial analysis, marketing and the other skills of modern business management were introduced to Irish entrepreneurs by organisations like the Irish Management Institute, and also by the new business and financial magazines that were introduced at this time.

In a sense one could argue that the division of labour was finally percolating through to the level of management itself. The technical experts in the public service had already proved their worth in the field of economic programming; the role of the professional administrator in Business and Labour organisation followed, and inevitably their style was different too from that of their predecessors, particularly so in Business. One prominent manager summed it up like this :

As a businessman employed in a private enterprise company which is owned by the shareholders, I have only one mandate . . . to increase the value of the shareholders' property.[7]

and again

A businessman managing an enterprise can only fully discharge his duty when he is making the largest possible profit.[8]

On the Labour front too, things changed somewhat. The new organisation and structure that was beginning to emerge is typified perhaps by the rise of the new Liberty Hall in Dublin, and in the largest unions at least, the attempt was made to provide a better quality of technical assistance to the representatives of Labour.

The trade unions solved their deepest rifts, but despite this, trade union officials continued to work under very difficult circumstances. The allocation of funds to paid officials, to research, to documentation and other essential aids continued to be minuscule in all but the largest unions. The work load continued to be very heavy, and one can only wonder at the dedication and industry of the few who served so well.

However, the fact remains that the unionisation of, for example, clerical workers in private employment did not make much progress, and inter-union difficulties continued to be major problems.

The Labour movement continued to be predominantly defensive in style, though not always in tone; the Labour dream of political as well as industrial progress was rebuffed electorally. The pragmatic approach triumphed, not only electorally, but in day-to-day affairs too.

The rise of this new technical stratum of administrator in Business and Labour organisations was badly needed, and it is of itself one of the most important developments since the war. The late Guy Jackson had put the point bluntly :

At this moment there are in this country fewer people than most of us would care to admit who have either the knowledge or indeed the assignment to understand and deal with all those complex economic issues which form the basis on which political decisions have to be made.[8]

The new importance of the skilled technical analyst is not of itself remarkable; rather the delay in his introduction to Ireland is perhaps more noteworthy. Nor is it surprising that such people found themselves deeply occupied in the many consultative committees which monitored and discussed and tried to implement the Second Programme. The institutional setting soon became largely tripartite, with the representatives of business, of labour and of government discussing the issues of employment, output, prices and trade. These discussions between the technical staffs of the social partners became, from the 1960s on, the prime arena in which Business and Labour played out their roles.

It did not matter greatly, it seems, which forum was being used, a broad consensus was pursued on most occasions. Once consensus was arrived at in committee, then inevitably it was hoped that the consensus view would also be accepted down the line, as it were, on the factory floor or in the company board room. The NIEC said:

> When representative bodies participate with government in reaching an agreed conclusion or decision, they must explicitly accept some responsibility for its implementation.[9]

Thus, the consultative arrangements in economic programming laid upon the representatives of Business and Labour weighty responsibilities, and raised the inevitable problem of the representative—his or her capacity to 'sell' the consensus view to those whom he or she represented. If the consultation procedures should become merely one-way channels of communication, then the vocational body being consulted, regardless of whether it be a trade union or employer organisation, becomes but an arm of central government. Once that happens, a dangerous threat to individual liberty and political democracy has emerged. Dangers such as these were spelled out much earlier by the Commission on Vocational Organisation:

> . . . a corporate state . . . takes . . . vocational bodies into the administrative and executive machinery of the State . . . [and] . . . (the) integration may be confined to economic planning or to a share in the formation of an economic council.[10]

Once decision-making is concentrated into the hands of the technical experts, then instead of according a high place to specialised skills, we are in danger of disenfranchising the un-skilled majority and of creating a semi-corporatist state. Tri-partite discussions are not of themselves necessarily corporatist; it may be argued that they are a feature of many Western countries. True, but it must be borne in mind that in most if not all these countries the highly centralised and integrated structure of Business and of Labour that is represented at the tripartite discussions is substantially offset by administrative structures at the level of the individual plan. Thereby workers have a direct input into the process of decision-making as it affects them most closely, through works councils, participatory structures or autonomous work group arrangements. In Ireland, and in the United Kingdom, this is not so. Here co-responsibility is frequently seen either as incipient sovietism or else as a sop to buy off militant workers.

The fact remains, though, that decisions made and handed down the line from higher to lower echelons frequently do not command loyalty or respect and are not always implemented with success.

In Ireland, particularly in the 1960s, the initiative of the public servants in presenting the First Programme has been generalised across the board into the organisation of Business and of Labour. There is now, it would seem, a real danger that the processes of decision-making on economic and social affairs have become too far removed from those most affected by them, and that they are concentrated in the hands of the specialist and the expert.

There are many ill-effects of such an eventuality, not least of them being that centralised decision-making tends to grow in-flexible as the problems confronting the decision-maker become more complicated; the recent experiences in Czechoslovakia and Hungary, not to mention the USSR itself, bear witness to this.

At another level however, if those rank and file members of trade unions or other such bodies become frustrated and alien-ated because they feel they no longer have any real say over the conditions of their daily working lives, then the dissatisfaction may well spill over in the form of wild-cat or otherwise inexplic-able industrial unrest. Professor O'Mahony some years ago commented on the increased importance of the shop steward on the factory floor and said:

This appears . . . partly the outcome of a possible deficiency in communications between the rank and file members of the trade unions and the full time officers.[11]

In general, however, the Labour movement has been reluctant to accept so dramatic a change in its role in society as is implied by a system of co-responsibility. Their present role was won after a difficult fight, and it is deeply prized. Labour has continued to defend itself not only against the employers, but also against other trade unions. It has continued to cast itself, and to be cast by society at large, as the defender of the union members, and as the continuing opposition in industrial politics, an opposition that does not aspire to govern in a factory coalition. Like William O'Brien, the organisation of Labour in Ireland has possessed 'in full measure courage, astuteness and determination, but not vision'.[12] If one criticises Labour organisations for being ideologically shortsighted, then, of course, so too was Business. At the outset of this chapter it was pointed out that in a market-based system, society responds to the divisions of labour by organising the interaction of the supply and demand for labour in a market. Such a mechanism, as O'Mahony has said 'cannot be expected to be an adequate basis of itself on which to build an undertaking considered as a community of persons'.[13]

Business has not wished to consider seriously the possibility of devolved decision-making, in whole or in part, at the level of the individual enterprise, but has retained instead a rigidly hierarchical structure. The replacement for the rather mawkish paternalism of some older family firms has been a view of job specialisation and human automation that is not really work study at all, but a vulgarisation of it. Ultimately, the dehumanisation of workers is counter-productive. Ivor Kenny wrote some time ago in terms that were, and are, rather far ahead of the Irish practice in business, or indeed elsewhere : '[employees] who are most talented will work only where they can satisfy their need for participation in their work beyond what is involved in the traditional weekly wage relationship',[14] but this view has not been taken to heart widely. The continuing failure to think in the longer term of the problems of the institutions of Business and Labour, and the failure in the post-war years to speculate on the roles which they might play in society, has been one of the great disappointments. To what can we attribute this failure of Business and Labour to build, in these otherwise constructive years, the framework for an industrial society at once democratic and flexible, at once economically developed and still human?

James Connolly is quoted as once saying that what we want is less philosophising and more fighting, and there are probably many who would agree with this view. The great watershed in Irish economic development after the war was undoubtedly the First Programme, and its philosophy was that economic growth could be engineered by re-directing existing talents and energies; no deep re-thinking was required, merely some ad hoc decisions and pragmatic choices, and all would be well. And so it was until the closing year or two of the 1960s. Irish society was not deeply disturbed ideologically, and the groundwork was not completed for sustained growth in the 1970s and subsequently. This is not to deny that very substantial progress was made, and for this we must all be grateful to those who led it and sustained it. But this questioning concerns the decision-making structure that has evolved for Business and Labour—does that structure have the firm democratic base to sustain the legitimacy of decisions taken, and the flexibility to make good decisions quickly? Or does it share in the inadequacies of much of centralised planning structures elsewhere? Has the pragmatism of the post-war reconstruction, which came very late in Ireland, by its very pragmatism given us now a framework that cannot be both efficient and democratic, but that tries to choose between the two?

NOTES

1. Plunket, James, 'Jim Larkin' in Boyle, J. W. (Ed.), *Leaders and Workers*, The Mercier Press, Cork.
2. See O'Mahony, D. P., *Economic Aspects of Industrial Relations*, The Economic Research Institute, Paper no. 24, Dublin 1965.
3. Whitaker, T. K., 'From Protection to Free Trade : The Irish Experience', *Administration*, vol. 21, no. 4, Winter 1973, 415.
4. *Capital Investment Advisory Committee: Third Report*, Government Publications, Dublin 1958.
5. *Economic Development*, Government Publications, Dublin 1958.

6. *Programme for Economic Expansion*, Government Publications, Dublin 1958.
7. Jackson, G. P., 'Private Enterprise in Action' at the National Management Conference, Killarney, 20–22 April 1967.
8. Jackson, G. P., *op. cit.*
9. Quoted by T. K. Whitaker in 'Economic Planning in Ireland, *Administration*, vol. 14, no. 4, Winter 1966, 283.
10. Commission on Vocational Organisation, *Report*, Government Publications, Dublin 1943, s. 15, 10, 11.
11. O'Mahony, D. P., *Industrial Relations: The Background*, The Economic Research Institute, Paper no. 19, Dublin 1964, 14.
12. Mitchell, Arthur, 'William O'Brien, 1881–1968, and the Irish Labour Movement', *Studies*, Autumn-Winter 1971, 330.
13. O'Mahony, D. P., ERI Paper no. 19, 2.
14. Kenny, Ivor, 'The Manager and Challenge of Change', *Irish Times*, 21 January 1969, 11.

The Farmers

Maurice Manning

On 7 October 1966, Rickard Deasy, President of the National Farmers' Association marshalled about sixteen followers around him in Bantry and with the blessing of the local Catholic priest and Protestant Minister and to the cheers of the fair-day crowd began the long march to Dublin, the centre of government and the home of the Department of Agriculture. Twelve days later Deasy was leading 30,000 farmers through the streets of Dublin towards that same Department. He was to find the way blocked and the Minister unwilling to see him. For twenty days and nights farmers' leaders sat, and slept, outside the Department as the government's attitude hardened and Sean Lemass, in his last days in office, talked of a 'small group of ambitious men' seeking to bully and intimidate the government, making arrogant demands which no government could concede.

The politics of confrontation had begun in earnest and the battle, often bitter and nasty, between farmers and government was to continue for the best part of a year. It was perhaps inevitable that some such confrontation would take place. Discontent had long been simmering in the farming community as farmers felt themselves left behind in the race for greater prosperity. Added to this was the fact that farmers in the past had benefited little from their participation in traditional party politics. The specifically farmers' parties of earlier decades had been unable to break established party loyalties and had rarely been little more than amateurs, easily squeezed out by the professionals. Thus from the 1950s on they had avoided party and parliamentary politics, organising instead into interest groups or pressure groups, seeking to build up the power and muscle to take on the government in the pursuit of their demands. And in this they had the example of their French, German and even British brothers who had taken to the streets and the roads, using direct action and disruptive methods to further their cause.

The NFA probably didn't win that particular battle in 1966/7. They didn't get all they were looking for and not only was the government still in office at the end of the day but it went on to win a further term of office in 1969. But, be that as it may, the events of 1966/7 clearly demonstrated that farmer power had arrived, that there was a new style of farmer politics and that in future all governments would have to take into account, along with organised labour and industry, the views of organised and militant agriculture.

In a way this point had been conceded by Sean Lemass in the Dáil in 1964 when he said that in future the government would welcome regular and full consultation with the NFA in the formulation of agricultural policy. But saying it was one thing, making it happen, another, and it was only after the events of 1966/7 that a note of urgency was injected into the whole process.

The events of 1966/7 are important because in one sense they were a preview of one aspect of the new politics of the late 1960s and early 1970s. Before long the public had become accustomed to seeing a variety of groups and causes taking to the street seeking their objectives—or at least publicity for them—through direct action. Neither were the lessons and tactics which the farmers had learned from their continental brothers lost on the other groups which resorted to direct tactics during this period—groups such as student housing action, and civil rights campaigners.

But from the farmers' point of view the events of 1966/7 were important, precisely because the tactics adopted then were *not* to become the norm. Neither was there to be a reversion to the parliamentary tactics of earlier decades. Instead when the heat of battle died down it was seen that the whole direction of farmer politics had changed, and instead of a continuation and escalation of the politics of confrontation, what emerged was a new emphasis on organisational efficiency, professional preparedness, publicity, public relation techniques and lobbying. What emerged too was an awareness that being part of the consultative process—or the new corporatism—was not enough on its own. Unless it could be accompanied by a high level of expertise and technical competence few battles could be won. And it was specifically the transformation of this awareness into reality which constitutes the real revolution in Irish farming politics. Within the space of ten years the NFA had acquired this expertise and gathered into its service a battery of experts in such areas as economics, sociology, agricultural science, public relations and communications.

Of course this transformation of the NFA was not occurring in isolation. Given the growth of consultation, both in principle and in practice by government departments other organisations were also finding that a growing level of technical preparedness was necessary. In addition the easier access to all sections of the media and the increasingly important role of the media in politics made such expertise doubly necessary. Thus other organisations began to develop along similar lines and for similar reasons—especially the trade unions and employers' organisations.

All of this is not to say that pressure groups or interest groups suddenly sprang into existence in the 1960s. Trade unions had been strong before the end of the nineteenth century, as had employers' organisations both general and specific. In the past, however, these organisations had few direct contacts with government. Unions negotiated with employers, either individually or in groups with the government firmly on the side-line. Nor did government seek to involve either in the formulation of policy or grant either a veto over policy. Kevin O'Higgins made no attempt to mollify the vintners who opposed his changes in the licensing laws. Patrick McGilligan publicly abused the Chambers of Commerce which attacked his Shannon Scheme. Sean MacEntee and Sean Lemass brusquely rejected the views of Bishops on questions of social and economic policy. True, the Bishops and the IMA did carry the day in the Mother and Child controversy, but that had been an exception. In general the attitude of governments to pressure groups had been somewhat dismissive, with little evidence of willingness to engage in dialogue. Indeed for some ministers a sign of strong government was a readiness to take on such groups and defeat them.

As has been noted, the late 1960s saw all that change as interest groups were consulted almost as of right by government departments and ministers in the formulation of public policy.

This new development was nothing more than a frank admission that in modern complex society government was easier and more likely to be successful if those groups which had power and a vested interest were consulted in advance of legislation, and, as far as possible, committed to agreement, also in advance.

These developments, while obviously marking an important advance in democratic consultation also contain dangers both for parliament and for the general public, and these will be touched upon later, but before doing that it is necessary to chart the evolution of the role of farmers within the political process.

Local farmers' unions existed before the foundation of the State and had occasionally been involved in local politics. After the foundation of the State and at a time when the party system was barely established, farmers' unions throughout the country decided to put forward candidates in various constituencies and to promote the interests of agriculture by establishing a Farmers' Party in the Dáil. In the 1922 elections seven of the thirteen farmers' candidates were elected while in the 1923 election there were sixty-five candidates out of whom fifteen were elected. The party continued to be represented throughout the 1920s.

It was never really a coherent political party with a national organisation. Its candidates were selected by the individual farmers' unions and its TDs tended to act more as independents than as members of a political party. Its policy was vague and generally negative—it opposed and constantly railed against government extravagance and waste: it was suspicious of civil servants, saw no need for a Department of External Affairs or for the ESB. It couldn't make up its mind on whether it was for free trade or protection and even on questions of agriculture had little that was constructive or positive to say.

In fairness the Farmers' Party might well have become more effective had it been given time to develop. Unfortunately for it the entry of Fianna Fáil to the Dáil in 1927 and the absence of an overall majority for any party forced it to take sides and from 1927 to 1932 it was in an informal coalition with the Cumann na nGaedhael government and its leader Michael Heffernan became Parliamentary Secretary to the Minister for Posts and Telegraphs.

In fact the Farmers' Party won only six seats in the September election of 1927 and its electoral experience was a clear indicator of the fate facing any independent or sectional group in the aftermath of the Civil War when, for most people, only one issue really mattered. In the existing political situation it was impossible *not* to take sides and for the Farmers Cumann na nGaelhael seemed a better guarantee of stable and conservative government. But taking sides inevitably alienated some supporters, blurred the party's own identity and eventually saw some of its members go the full way and join the Cosgrave party.

The next attempt at a farmers' party sought to build on a broader base. The attempt however was to prove short-lived. This was the Centre Party of James Dillon and Frank Mac-Dermott which after just a year in existence found itself unable to stay out of the Civil War quarrel, and along with the Blueshirts became a founding part of Fine Gael in 1933.

It wasn't for another ten years that the next farmers' party emerged—this time the Clann na Talmhan party which won twelve seats in the 1943 election. This party was essentially a populist protest on the part of smaller farmers in depressed areas. It never had any central organisation and its policies were neither detailed nor particularly imaginative. Its appearance was a symptom of the frustration and impotence of small farmers, who felt themselves ignored and misunderstood by a remote government and bureaucracy and exploited by big business and rapacious unions.

After its initial impact Clann na Talmhan had to face much the same dilemma as the earlier farmers' parties. In the Dáil the Civil War issue was as alive as ever and the new party had to find a way of exerting influence without taking sides. But of course they were forced to take sides—voting against the Fianna Fáil Government, on many occasions between 1943–48 and then participating in the two interparty governments.

This participation was sincere and well-intentioned but it can hardly be said that it achieved much more for the farmers than would have been the case had Fianna Fáil been in power. Eventually the Clann na Talmhan party was to splutter out in the mid-1960s. But before that happened another development— and much more significant though less newsworthy at the time— was taking place.

This was the foundation of the Young Farmer movement in

1944 at a time when rural morale could hardly have been worse. It was a time of low incomes, high emigration and endemic shortages. Most of all it was time of little hope—before even the ESB's campaign of rural electrification had begun to transform life in the countryside.

The Young Farmer Clubs originated in Athy in 1944, and the honour of founding the movement belongs to the late Stephen Cullinane, a young agricultural science teacher. The clubs developed around discussion groups usually led by agricultural advisers and rural science teachers. In spite of the apathy and defeatism of the time the movement spread rapidly from three clubs at the end of 1944 to 350 clubs by the end of 1950 and close on 500 clubs by the time of its tenth anniversary. And long before then the name of Young Farmers Clubs had been replaced by Macra na Feirme.

The impact of Macra na Feirme on the morale of rural areas is difficult to estimate but it was considerable and even from the perspective can be seen as one of the most positive and constructive movements ever to be founded in Ireland. Especially important was the fact that from the start it began to involve itself not just in major policy matters, but in the detail of agricultural policy, and did so in an organised and systematic way. In 1949 it appointed a full-time general secretary—later its first chief executive—Mr Sean Healy and it also appointed a part-time economic adviser, Professor Louis Smith.

Macra na Feirme must be unique among organisations in that it realised that if it continued to develop at the pace it was developing it would lose much of its original purpose and character. So instead of trying to do everything itself it helped bring into existence two new organisations specifically geared to look after the economic interests of the Irish farmer.

In May 1950 it helped found the Irish Creamery Milk Suppliers' Association at Kilmallock in the heart of the intensive dairying counties. From the start the ICMSA was a militant agitating organisation, concerned mainly with those who produced milk for manufacturing purposes. In 1953 it conducted the first milk strike in the country—a strike which lasted sixteen days and in the end was judged a success because the farmers got an increase of $1\frac{3}{4}$d per gallon for their milk. Even more significant was the emergence of new methods—direct methods, even the strike weapon, hitherto the preserve of the trade unions.

A year later, in 1954, Macra was to play an even more direct role in bringing a new organisation into existence, this time the National Farmers' Association which was launched at an enthusiastic meeting in Dublin in January 1955. The NFA brought with it much of the expertise Macra had been building up on economic and policy matters and right from the start it was clear that the brunt of the bargaining on behalf of farmers would henceforth be carried by the NFA.

First, however, there was the question of farming unity. The ICMSA was only one of a number of commodity organisers which feared the possibility of a take-over by the NFA. After a long series of negotiations, chaired initially by Bishop Lucey of Cork, it was clear that the basis for unity did not exist. Eventually the two main organisations, the NFA and the ICMSA then agreed to work separately though it must be said that relations between the two organisations were less than friendly. Indeed at times the relationship was to be characterised by personality clashes and considerable bitterness.

The influence of the NFA spread rapidly in the years after its foundation, especially in such things as the pioneering of livestock marts, bovine TB eradication and in a generally more aggressive championing of farmers' issues. But it was not until 1964 that the NFA received formal government recognition when Sean Lemass told the Dáil that in future the government would welcome regular and full discussions and consultation with the NFA in the formulation of agricultural policy, both broad and specific. Henceforth he said it would be normal government policy that the Minister for Agriculture would, in advance, inform the NFA of any proposed changes in government policy and that there would be an annual review of the whole agricultural situation in which the NFA would be fully involved.

It was an important milestone in the history of the NFA but it was not enough to stave off the growing tide of farmer discontent and anger. This discontent was due to the strong belief that farmers were being left very much behind in the growing prosperity of the 1960s, and was fuelled by an equally strong conviction, sometimes amounting to a certainty, that the bureaucrats in Dublin simply didn't understand or care enough about their problems, or were too remote to do anything about them.

As has been mentioned the NFA's campaign to focus attention on their demands began dramatically in Bantry on 7 October 1966. The *Irish Times* of the following day reported it thus: 'The tide of agrarian discontent this morning rolled out from the damp but sunny centre of Bantry. That tide as it progresses will wash around the Department of Agriculture in Dublin on 19 October. But this morning for the 16 men, the first of the NFA "Farmers Rights Marchers" who face a 217 mile walk Dublin seemed, and indeed was a long way away'.

The marchers were led by Rickard Deasy—a Tipperary farmer, but hardly a typical one. He had been educated at Oxford and Louvain and had served in the Irish army during the Emergency. Over the next few weeks his military appearance, his stout stick and beret were to make him look more like a paramilitary leader than the rather quiet Tipperary farmer he is. And as he flashed onto television screens or appeared on the front pages of the papers Rickard Deasy seemed to symbolise the new militancy and stridency of Irish farmers using a language which demanded rather than asked. The march grew in size and volume with each passing day. As it passed through towns and villages it generated a sense of enthusiasm and created an air of expectancy and excitement hitherto unknown among the farming community. At the start of the march Mr Deasy had placed it under the protection of Pope John, a current symbol of social justice. Before long at least two Bishops, Dr O'Callaghan from Clogher and Dr Ryan of Clonfert had given their support. Not so enthusiastic were the many motorists inconvenienced by the march which in some cases seemed to exacerbate traditional town-country rivalries. More important the sometimes inflammatory statements of Mr Deasy and his cohorts ensured that the already hard line of the government would be harder still. The Minister for Agriculture Mr Haughey refused to meet the NFA leaders who then began a sit-down protest outside the Minister's offices in a mood of engulfing ill-will, distrust and bad temper. Over the next few weeks Mr Haughey bore the brunt of the farmers' anger—he was jostled by farmers in Merrion Street, called a 'rat' by other farmers in Ballsbridge, had his car attacked in Athlone and, perhaps worst of all, was threatened with the withdrawal of hunting rights by some farmers over whose lands he hunted.

The government line however remained adamant. To give in would be to abdicate responsibility and Sean Lemass steeled his colleagues to resist. In the event Mr Haughey did not meet the NFA, though a face-saving compromise was found. However it was no more than that—a compromise, not a solution, and the battle continued, erupting again in early 1967.

This time the bitterness was more intense and actions on both sides were more extreme. On 6 January 1967, the twelfth anniversary of the foundation of the NFA, farmers throughout the country blocked roads with their cars, tractors and farm machinery, bringing all traffic to a standstill. Later when farmers were prosecuted many refused to pay their fines. The situation was quickly coming to resemble the Economic War of thirty years earlier and in the farming folk memory that was little more than yesterday. Once again farmers were going to jail, becoming local martyrs in the process and steeling the resolve of their colleagues to resist. And in such circumstances rumours were rife, especially the rumour that the government was about to proscribe the NFA and make it an illegal organisation.

Again just as had happened in the Economic War, farmers refused to pay their local rates. And, just as in the past, Gardai moved in to seize their property, though it was alleged at the time (and with justification) that the farmers selected were usually the wealthiest and the goods seized usually conspicuous consumer goods so that urban viewers watching the events on television would not have too much sympathy for the suffering farmers.

Another tactic tried was a commodity strike which in spite of considerable farmer solidarity was hardly a success. By May the campaign showed no signs of abating. In that month there were 100 farmers in jail and there were mass rallies outside Portlaoise Prison, including a demonstration of 2,000 farm women.

However by June 1967 tempers had begun to cool down. The new Taoiseach, Mr Jack Lynch met a delegation of farming women. Later the jailed farmers were released and the relations began to return to some sort of normality. Indeed, the surprising thing in retrospect is how little bitterness was to remain. In a way both sides had made their point and learned their lesson. Government realised that it could not afford *not* to consult fully with the farmers while the farmers got an accurate measure of their own strength—they could put pressure on government and they could make life difficult for them— but they were not going to dictate. Both sides learned that in the politics of confrontation there are rarely any real winners.

The years after 1967 were to be years of rapid change and sustained growth for the NFA or, as it later became, The Irish Farmers' Association (IFA). Under the leadership of Rickard Deasy and later T. J. Maher the public voice of the organisation was to be aggressive and strident. Its leaders made clear their determination to fight for the interests of their members, to use every available weapon and to care little if the public image of the farming community was to arouse the hostility of urban dwellers.

But behind this public stridency—undoubtedly accentuated by easy and frequent access to radio and television—both the structure and operating methods of the NFA were changing. Farming was becoming big business and with Ireland's accession to the EEC it would become bigger still. The Common Agricultural Policy promised rewards undreamt of a decade earlier. In this new situation technocratic competence was more likely to prove effective than populist pressure though that too could still have its uses.

The NFA thus had every incentive to organise. And in a sense the groundwork had been done in the old Macra na Feirme days when the need for expertise had been clearly spelled out and accepted. The events of 1966/7 had strengthened farming solidarity, established strong bonds between leaders and members and created a real sense of identity. Thus on this basis, with such an incentive and in the new political climate, the NFA developed into what it is today, one of the most effective and sophisticated pressure groups of its kind in Europe. It has adapted to the changed and pressurised conditions of the EEC better than any other Irish organisation. Its research, expertise and public relations is as good, if not better than, most government departments. It generally knows what it wants, what is in the interests of its members, and it knows where and how to make its case.

All of this development has taken place over a comparatively

C

short period of time. What it means is that the farmers' organisations, like the unions and business—only better than either—
have adapted to the realities of power and the exercise of power
in a modern quasi-corporate State.

These developments were not of course unique to Ireland.
What was happening here had many parallels in other developed
and developing countries. Moreover it is a trend which is
likely to continue over the coming years and it is something
which raises some new and fundamental questions for a democratic society. So far these questions are barely being asked, let
alone answered, not just here but elsewhere as well.

The first question is that of accountability. Pressure groups,
invariably work *outside* of the electoral process, and are concerned with specific interests rather than any general interest
and are accountable only to those they serve, even though
their activities may have widespread and far-reaching consequences throughout society generally. In some ways the more
sectional and self-interested a group is, the more it will be
regarded as successful by its members. As has been observed,
the same process which brings the interested groups into consultation shuts the general public out of it.

There is no evidence to suggest any improper behaviour on
the part of interest groups in Ireland. That however is not the
case in such countries as the USA or Germany and there is little
doubt that with the growing scale of interest group activities
and the very large amounts of money involved, abuses may
occur here also. The question of some form of regulation and
scrutiny of interest group activity is one which parliament may
have to face up to in the near future.

Secondly there is the consequence for parliament itself of
the growth in pressure group strength and activity. The more
these groups are consulted the more parliament finds itself
isolated and irrelevant, with neither the will nor the muscle
to demand that it be properly consulted or indeed even be
taken into account at all on other than purely formal matters.

What is being said here applies to virtually all modern parliaments and indeed it has long been fashionable to talk about the
decline of parliament which itself presupposes that parliament
formerly played a powerful and central role in the framing of
legislation. Whether this assumption is true or not the fact is

today that parliament, and its members, have become largely irrelevant to the formulation of public policy; they can talk about it, they can vote for it or against as dictated by their party, but in the end the details, and the principles of what they are voting for or against, have already been hammered out elsewhere, after the real bargaining and consultation with the interest groups and the bureaucrats.

One of the most striking aspects of Irish politics over the past two decades has been the growth of party professionalism, especially in such aspects as campaigning and public relations techniques. But this same period which has seen the emergence of a variety of strong professional pressure groups has seen no growth whatsoever in the ability of parliament to perform its basic functions. This growth in professional competence which has been such a feature of most aspects of Irish life in this period has left parliament virtually untouched. It is not just that salaries and facilities for research and information are bad —which they are. Much more serious is the docile acceptance of the situation by the majority of deputies of all parties, with little or no realisation of the exent to which the Oireachtas has become a side-show to the real decision-making process which now involves cabinet, pressure group and EEC officials. And perhaps the most disturbing feature of all is the fact that no attempt has been made by politicians here to learn from the experience of other countries and other parliaments which have had to face this same problem especially those countries which have tackled it in a serious way and with some degree of success such as, perhaps, Sweden and West Germany.

It may well be that the experience of participating in the European Parliament with its elaborate system of committees, consultation and research services will open the eyes of Irish parliamentarians to new possibilities. Maybe too the increasing number of full-time, and generally better educated politicians will wake up to the fact of their present irrelevance, to the pointlessness of so much of what they are asked to do, and out of these frustrations will come a genuine move for greater parliamentary involvement in the work of government.

And yet there is no sign of this happening, which leads to the general observation that the period under review—post-war Ireland—has not been a happy or auspicious one for parliament and parliamentary democracy. What we have seen is an enormous growth in the scope and complexity of government. We have seen an impressive growth of professionalism and expertise and an unprecedented degree of consultation between governors and governed.

But more and more this consultation is taking place outside of parliament, involving the pressure groups who have become the real powers in Irish society over the past quarter century, and without whose consent effective government is not possible. The farmers are the most spectacular but by no means the only example of this phenomenon which has changed the power balance within Irish society and which has raised questions and problems which have yet to be resolved.

Education and Society in Ireland, 1945-70

John Sheehan

The Irish educational system in 1945 was in many respects similar to that inherited by the State at its independence, with few changes either in structure or on policy objectives since the 1920s. It combined decentralisation of the ownership and management of most schools with a very high degree of centralisation of financial control, curriculum, inspection and examination in the hands of the Department of Education. There had been no noteworthy change in the system since the 1930 Vocational Education Act, nor was there to be any until the 1960s.

Following the upheaval of the war years, there was throughout Europe in the late 1940s a considerable degree of social and economic reform, which affected educational systems—for example the 1944 Education Act had introduced free secondary education for all in England and Wales. Commitments to full employment and economic growth would by themselves have produced considerable expansion, but the additional aspiration of equality of educational opportunity was a further source of change. In particular, it became policy in most countries to lower as far as possible the financial barriers to educational participation faced by low income families, and increasing emphasis was placed on educational institutions which were comprehensive in curriculum and outlook and which did not introduce rigid distinctions between academic education and technical training at an early age.

However, it is clear that these developments largely by-passed the Ireland of the 1940s and 1950s and the period 1945 to 1962 is, by contrast to what happened later, one of stagnation. While there was investment in new school buildings, and while secondary school enrolments doubled (the school-age population rose only about 7 per cent),[1] institutional structures, curricula, and general education policies hardly changed at all. Enrolment grew more because of rising parental expectations for their children and rising real incomes rather than because of deliberate acts of policy. The relatively small number of scholarships is sufficient proof of this. Furthermore, in the case of the universities, where student numbers increased by a half during the 1950s, the lack of any significant expansion of facilities produced overcrowding of serious proportions.[2]

The outlook of educationists during the 1950s is amply illustrated by the reports of the Council of Education, an official advisory body of thirty-one members mainly representing teachers and school authorities, which functioned from 1950 to 1962, producing reports on the curricula of the Primary and Secondary School.

The Council's 1962 report on secondary schools[3] offers a particularly sharp contrast to the many reforms which, as we shall see, were instituted shortly after its publication. The principle objective of education was stated to be the religious, moral and cultural development of the child. It was pretty clear that the social and economic aspects of this development— that is the relation of socio-economic background to educational attainment and the relation between education and subsequent opportunities—were largely ignored. Indeed there was an implicit hostility to such considerations, as in the statement that 'in general the aim of science teaching in the secondary school is cultural rather than practical'.

The Council went on to recommend *against* the state-financing or ownership of new secondary school buildings, publicly-financed vocational guidance schemes and the abolition of fees.[4] Secondary education for all was seen as utopian on both financial and educational grounds. Any positive recommendations were concerned with the details of individual subjects in the curriculum. Any fundamental changes were dismissed and the reasons given were almost invariably not based on empirical evidence. It may seem unusual to place such emphasis on the reports of such a forgotten body as the Council of Education, but in its deductivist approach to analysing problems, its deference to the status quo, and its isolation of educational issues from their wider social context, it is an almost perfect reflection of much contemporary educational thinking.

The period from 1963 to 1970 was, however, to make up for the stagnation of the earlier years, if only for the almost bewildering number of developments in official policy. Once again an official report is important—in this case both because it provided so much information on how the educational system worked and also because it raised issues which have ever since preoccupied those concerned with Irish education. This report, entitled *Investment in Education*, was quite significantly the production of a small expert working body rather than a large unwieldy council or commission.[5] It was also sponsored by the Organisation for Economic Co-operation and Development and marked the influence of ideas from abroad on educational policy. *Investment in Education* focused on three main themes:

1. Education and the manpower requirements of the economy.
2. Effective use of educational resources.
3. The proportions of various socio-economic groups who 'drop out' of the system at different stages.

It also emphasised the links which exist within and between the various levels of the system: such an overall view of the educational system would, of course, be an important aspect of educational planning.

The usefulness of a small expert team is highlighted when one contrasts *Investment in Education* with the report of the *Commission on Higher Education*.[6] The Commission, which was of the traditional broadly-based type, sat from 1960 to 1967. Some important policy decisions were made without waiting for its report, and the subsequent direction of expansion at the third level was much more towards the technological area than it recommended. It would seem that in the Irish context councils or commissions of enquiry which comprise a representative group of educationists either play safe by opting for the status quo, or have any new recommendations so hedged about by qualifications and reservations that their impact is considerably diminished.

When one examines the working of the component parts of the educational system it becomes apparent that about 1963 there occurred a general change in emphasis, away from purely educational and language revival questions and towards the social and economic dimensions.

At the primary level, national schools are the most important institution, as over 95 per cent of all pupils pass through them. Between 1945 and 1962 there was little change in curriculum and a modest increase in enrolment—about 7 per cent over fifteen years. By earlier standards there was considerable investment in new school buildings, but the result by 1963/64 was still a system of buildings which were in many respects extremely primitive and in bad repair, as *Investment in Education* has shown. For example, less than half of all schools had piped drinking water and modern sanitation.[7] One cannot put the entire blame for this on the managerial system; bureaucratic delays in replacing buildings and an inadequate public budgetary allocation were the prime factors.

By the mid-1960s, two factors combined to force a change in policy. First, increasing numbers put a lot of pressure on resources—especially on the current and prospective supply of qualified teachers.[8] Secondly, the *Investment in Education* report had shown how small rural schools were not only very often in need of repair or replacement, they were also very costly in terms of current resources—which meant teachers— without any obvious offsetting educational or economic benefit.[9] The ever present problem of national schools was (and is) the number of large classes. While the *average* pupil-teacher ratio of about 33 : 1 may not have seemed large, the dispersion of class sizes about this average was considerable. Large numbers of small rural schools had pupil-teacher ratios of less than 20 : 1 while at the other extreme many urban schools had ratios in excess of 40 : 1 with individual classes often in excess of 50.[10]

The policy of amalgamation of the small schools introduced in the mid-1960s made sense, although perhaps understandably there was some local opposition at first. Fewer teachers were needed in sparsely populated rural areas, leaving more available for the growing needs of the towns. The schools which were closed were generally those which were most in need of repair and would have needed considerable money spent on them in any event. There were extra costs notably in the provision of free transport, but a similar scheme for secondary pupils made this a more viable proposition.

The result of this rationalisation of school building was a very significant improvement in basic physical conditions :

heating, lighting, sanitation.[11] In addition, more comprehensive provision of school libraries and audio-visual aids (almost unknown in the 1950s) became possible. In later years this would facilitate the introduction of a new and wider curriculum and also teaching methods which were more in line with those prevailing in other countries.

At the second level, the privately-owned and managed secondary schools contained about 75 per cent of all full-time pupils during the 1945–62 period; the other 25 per cent were in vocational schools, doing a Group Certificate Course which did not qualify for further full-time education beyond the age of 15 or 16. While secondary schools' running costs were subsidised, all their capital costs had to be met from private sources. This system had its achievements: it catered for a doubling of enrolments in the years 1945 to 1963; it managed to keep fees at an exceedingly modest level and to remit them entirely in many cases; and it resulted in a greater degree of educational participation by 15 and 16 year olds than the largely free systems of the United Kingdom. But there were severe deficiencies, some of them obvious, other highlighted by *Investment in Education*.[12] Considerable numbers did not complete even their primary schooling, and many 14 year old school leavers had never transferred from primary to post-primary schools. The children of manual workers (especially the unskilled) had very low participation rates in second-level education. There was a high dropout rate from Intermediate Certificate and especially Group Certificate courses, and very few pupils from the latter course ever got a third level education. Finally, some areas were inadequately served by secondary schools, partly due to low population density.

A series of measures, which was aimed at rectifying some of these deficiencies, was taken even before *Investment in Education* was published, and some of these were later to assume great significance. In May 1963, the Minister for Education, Dr Hillery, announced a decision to build a small number of comprehensive state-owned schools in areas with inadequate secondary facilities, as well as a common Intermediate Certificate course for all schools, thus putting vocational school courses on a more equal basis. Further measures were to follow in the subsequent three years: more comprehensive schools, more scholarships, schemes for co-operation between vocational and secondary schools (which contained the first hint of the community school idea), and public funds for secondary school building. The latter was of considerable importance as it would ultimately give the authorities control over the future size and location of the privately-owned secondary schools.[13]

Though these changes were individually quite small and seemingly unco-ordinated, they had considerable effect. Enrolments increased more rapidly—at nearly 5,000 a year after 1963 compared to about 3,600 a year between 1957 and 1962. A series of small changes did not necessitate lengthy negotiations with various interest groups; the changes could be gradually enlarged and extended presenting these groups with a series of *faits accomplis* which might otherwise have been impossible. The more the system was expanded by a judicious extension of subsidies, the more the greatest power in the hands of the Department of Education—the power of the purse-strings—was brought to bear.

In discussing these developments which were to culminate in the O'Malley 'free education' plan of 1966, one further factor must be mentioned : the decision to raise the minimum school-leaving age to 15 by 1970, first revealed in the *Second Programme for Economic Expansion*.[14] This could hardly be done simply by 'tacking on' another year to the national school programme. Universal education to age 15 meant some type of second level education for all, and universal *compulsory* education was hardly compatible with the payment of fees. Hence there was an implicit commitment to some kind of radical change at the second level pre-existing the O'Malley plan by three years.

Nevertheless, the O'Malley scheme caused a sensation when it did arise, and the manner of its announcement in 1967 was in itself controversial.[15] Straightforward abolition of the small fees in comprehensive and vocational schools was proposed, and while all secondary schools would continue to receive existing grants, a special supplementary grant was to be paid to those schools which undertook to charge no fees. Free transport was to be provided for pupils living more than three miles from the nearest school. For Protestant schools, because of their different cost structures, a lump sum was to be provided to the school authorities, which when administered on a means-test basis, was calculated to provide effective remission of fees for 75 per cent of all pupils. Pupils in Catholic schools did not have to submit to any means test; however, distinctions would inevitably arise between fee-paying and 'free' schools.

The immediate effect of the O'Malley scheme was dramatic. Enrolments increased by 18,000 in 1967 alone, and by over 10,000 per annum in the ensuing four years. Over 90 per cent of secondary pupils—instead of the original estimate of 75 per cent—were in schools opting into the free scheme. However, when the direct impact of free education should have run its course in 1971, enrolments continued to rise at a very high rate. In due course rising population was to have a cumulatively greater impact than any single policy measure such as the abolition of fees.

Third level education in Ireland has traditionally been over-whelmingly concentrated in the universities. During the 1950s the considerable expansion in student numbers was not matched by increased accommodation, so in the following decade very large investments were undertaken, both to make up for the deficiences and to cater for further growth. Initially, this invest-ment was not matched by planning or by definite ideas about the required size and structure of the system as a whole; for example, only *after* much of the new UCD Belfield campus was either built or in progress, was the question raised of a UCD/TCD merger or co-ordination of some sort, and the Belfield scheme was by far the biggest single educational build-ing programme ever financed by the Irish Government. The overcrowding in the mid-1960s was so severe that it was not possible to wait for the Commission on Higher Education to report—and when it did report many of its recommendations were never implemented. The establishment of a Higher Edu-cation Authority did, however, produce more orderly develop-ment after 1968, but the Authority suffers from the limitation of having direct responsibility for only some designated institu-tions.[16] What is in some respects surprising is that the federal NUI structure—a structure which in the opinion of many has become increasingly unwieldy with the growing complexity of the constituent university colleges—has remained intact. Simi-larly, Trinity College has been changed much more by a Catholic episcopal decision—the removal of the ban on attendance by Catholics—than by any government legislation. As in other parts of the educational system, the absence of any legislation which defines or alters the status and powers of educational institutions is quite remarkable.

The really important developments in third level education in the 1960s occurred in the technological sector, and they continue to have a large impact on the growth of technological education today. Apart from a doubling of the number of full-time students in the Dublin Colleges of Technology between 1965 and 1970, two new types of institution were founded. A National Institute of Higher Education in Limerick provided degree and diploma courses largely in the commercial and technological areas, and a network of Regional Technical Colleges was established in major centres throughout the country.[17] These colleges, which engage in both second and third level work, have displayed considerable flexibility in meeting local needs and have provided a range of technical courses previously unavailable outside Dublin. The growth in fulltime student numbers in the technological sector is worth noting: 850 in 1965, 1,700 in 1970, and over 6,000 in 1976—half of them in the Regional Colleges.

In addition, the vocational and technological sectors have continued to expand their part-time and adult education courses. Over the years, apprentice training has become more integrated with technical education, and recently, it has become the responsibility of AnCo—the Industrial Training Authority. From almost nothing ten years ago industrial training has become a major activity; strictly speaking it is not part of the educational system, but in practice close co-operation exists between AnCo and vocational and technological education authorities.

Turning to the overall financial impact of all these developments there is, as one might expect, a pronounced break in the figures in the years immediately following 1963. Money figures are rendered meaningless because of inflation; instead we will consider education's share of GNP and of government expenditure. In the twenty years between 1945 and 1964 public education expenditure was about 3 per cent of GNP—private spending is difficult to estimate but it was probably between 0.50 and 1 per cent. Between 1964 and 1970 the share of education rose to $5\frac{1}{2}$ per cent and reached $6\frac{1}{2}$ per cent by 1975.

Similarly, education's share of total government spending rose between 1964 and 1970 from about 9 per cent to 12 per cent, having shown a declining trend in the previous twenty years.[18] Are these changes the result of policy developments which we have been describing or are they due to some other autonomous cause? While total enrolments in education rose by 200,000 in the years 1963 to 1975 when education's share of GNP doubled, about 85 per cent of the increase in numbers was accounted for by the under 15s, and this points to demographic factors as having a major influence on the size and structure of the educational system. That growth in population and the labour force which a previous essay (Brendan Walsh on 'Economic Growth and Development, 1945–70') in this volume has concluded is a major problem for employment policy in the 1970s and 1980s has already had quite dramatic effects on the educational system.

In educational terms, the largest single change has been the universalisation of second level schooling consequent on raising the school-leaving age and on the O'Malley free education scheme. Whereas even in 1963 about one-third of an age group left school with only primary education and another third with no post-primary certificate of any kind, by the early 1970s some post-primary education was becoming almost the universal rule. This changed the primary schools: their pupils transferred out at an earlier age. It also produced increased pressures on the higher levels of the system in due course.

Did these changes lead to greater equality of educational opportunity or of attainment? It has often been argued that the greatest benefits from free education go to the middle class; and this is probably true, if educational reform goes no further than the simple abolition of fees. The increasing demands from the teaching profession for more remedial education are probably indicative of something similar. But most important, educational researchers in many countries have found that educational inequalities begin at an early age and are conditioned by family background to a very large extent. For Ireland, Kathleen Cullen's 1969 study[19] of educational retardation among 11 to 14 year olds confirms this: parental education, parental aspiration—or rather their absence—are very strongly associated with educational problems in children. Free secondary education will not solve these problems, and still less will increased students' grants lead to any radical equalisation of access to higher education. While it was inevitable that primary schools would account for a much diminished share of the educational budget —about 35 per cent in 1970 compared to 70 per cent in 1945, perhaps only an increased priority for primary schools, a partial reversal of this trend, can go to the root of the problem of greater equality in education.

To some, the advances in the 1960s in Irish education are associated with disputes between the Department of Education, the schools, the churches, the teachers' unions and other interest groups. No one in authority has ever been willing or able to formally change the inherited structures : a look at the turbulent history of education in the nineteenth century gives one plenty of reasons for that. But beneath all the interest-group conflict there has been solid progress, in the spread of education, in the professionalism of educators and in the conduct of research. The unquestioning adherence to dogma, best illustrated by earlier attitudes to revival of Irish, has been replaced by work such as McNamara's investigation of the effects of bilingualism,[20] with its emphasis on empirical investigation and its general premise that the individual child rather than national policies are the centre of educational concern. These changes as well as social and economic developments which surround them are all part of the transformation of Irish society which began in the early 1960s, and which is still continuing.

NOTES

1. Of course this implies considerable increases in enrolment *rates* (i.e. percentage of an age-group enrolled in full-time education). Most of the figures quoted here are from Department of Education annual reports (which in recent years have been confined to statistical information), see *Tuarascáil Staitistiúil* (Stationery Office, Dublin, Annual 1945 to 1970, then 1969/70 to 1971/72, 1972/73 and 1973/74, 1974/75 and 1975/76). A useful summary of the statistical information up to 1962/63 is found in vol. 2 of *Investment in Education* (Stationery Office, Dublin 1966, Pr. 8527).
2. See the *Report of Commission on Accommodation Needs of*

NUI Constituent Colleges (Stationery Office, Dublin 1959, Pr. 5089).

3. Council of Education, *The Curriculum of the Secondary School* (Dublin, Stationery Office, 1962, Pr. 5996).
4. *Op. cit.*, 82, 252–4.
5. Vol. I, Dublin Stationery Office, 1965, Pr. 8311, vol. II 1966, Pr. 8527.
6. *Commission on Higher Education, 1960–67*, Report. Part I (Pr. 9326); Part II, vol 1 (Pr. 9389); Part II, vol 2 (Pr. 9588), Dublin, Stationery Office, 1967.
7. *Op. cit.*, vol. I, 247–52.
8. Between 1958 and 1964 the number of births increased by $7\frac{1}{2}$ per cent. More important the numbers aged 5–14 rose from 542,000 in 1951 to 576,000 in 1961, 584,000 in 1966 and 615,000 by 1971. (All census of population figures.)
9. Average current costs per pupil in one-teacher schools were more than three times as high as in large schools with seven or more teachers. See *Investment in Education*, vol. I, Table 9.10, 237.
10. In 1962/63 the average pupil-teacher ratio (and therefore average class size) in one-teacher schools was 17. At the other extreme 23.3 per cent of all pupils (i.e. about 114,000) were in classes of over 50 pupils. See *Investment in Education*, vol. I, 234. Rapid progress in the elimination of very large classes did not come until the mid-1970s.
11. Unpublished Departmental surveys of National School facilities have been undertaken in recent years. Some information from the 1972 survey is given in the National Economic and Social Council *Educational Expenditure in Ireland* (Report No. 12, Dublin Stationery Office, 1975, Pr. 4730), Table 3.1, 58.
12. See especially vol. I, ch. 6.
13. For an account of these changes see E. Randles, *Post Primary Education in Ireland, 1957–1970* (Veritas, Dublin, 1975) especially ch. 5–8.
14. *Second Programme for Economic Expansion,* Part II (Stationery Office, Dublin, 1964, Pr. 7670), ch. 8, 198.
15. There was some doubt as to whether the manner of announcement constituted a breach of collective cabinet responsibility, especially as there was a considerable commitment of public funds apparently without the involvement of the Minister of Finance. On this see B. Farrell's study of the office of Taoiseach, *Chairman or Chief* (Gill and Macmillan, Dublin, 1971), especially 69–70.

16. The Authority functioned as an *ad hoc* body from 1968 to 1972, when it was formally constituted under the *Higher Education Authority Act 1971*. While the Authority has a general role in assessing resource needs for all higher education it has direct financial responsibility in controlling the flow of resources to a limited number of 'designated' institutions—mainly the Universities until very recently.

17. There are nine Regional Technical Colleges, in Athlone, Carlow, Cork, Dundalk, Galway, Letterkenny, Sligo, Tralee and Waterford.

18. Education's share of government spending does not show the same dramatic rise as its share of national spending. This is because government expenditure itself has accounted for a rising share of GNP since the early 1960s.

19. K. Cullen, *School and Family: Social factors in educational attainment*, Dublin, Gill and Macmillan, 1969.

20. J. MacNamara, *Bilingualism and Primary Education: A Study of Irish Experience*, Edinburgh University Press, 1966.

Church, State and Society, 1950-70

John Whyte

Irish Catholicism at the beginning of the 1950s seemed very different from today. The dominant tone was what has since come to be called 'triumphalism'. To read the Catholic press, one would hardly guess that the Church had any problems. There was scarcely a hint of disagreement among Catholics, still less of there being parties in the Church. Ecclesiastical news seemed like an unbroken round of successes—churches built, missions established, congresses held. True, there were a few dissenting voices. A little periodical called *The Bell* published critical articles on the role of the Church in Ireland. But it appeared irregularly, and disappeared altogether in 1954. The main alternative voice was provided by the *Irish Times*, which offered a forum for differing views in its correspondence columns, and even on one occasion—at the time of the mother-and-child-scheme crisis—criticised the bishops in its editorial. But it had a small circulation, appealing to a particular segment of the population. The other three dailies—the *Irish Independent*, the *Irish Press*, and the *Cork Examiner*—were totally circumspect, as was Radio Éireann. Telefís Éireann, of course, did not then exist.

In so far as controversy did occur during these years, it arose because some churchmen and zealous laymen, felt that Ireland was not Catholic enough. The early 1950s marked the high-water-mark in Ireland of the Catholic social movement. This movement had begun on the continent in the late nineteenth century, and its ideas had been worked out by continental theologians. Irish Catholics had had almost no share in its development, and had not shown much interest in it until the 1930s. But once they took it up, they imported its theories with uncritical enthusiasm. From the 1940s there was a whole bevy of interlocking groups—An Rioghacht, the Christus Rex Society, the Guilds of Regnum Christi, and others—dedicated to reshaping Ireland on the lines laid down by Catholic social principles.

What were these principles? There were two main ones, a negative and a positive. The negative one was a distrust of state power. The state was felt as a dangerous force. Any attempt to strengthen it could lead to totalitarianism. This was an understandable fear at a time when Hitler was a recent memory and Stalin was still alive, but it was taken so far that even a welfare state on the British model was looked on with suspicion: Cardinal D'Alton of Armagh condemned it in his lenten pastoral for 1952. The positive principle was that society should be built up on the basis of vocational groups. Vocational groups were a combination of all those working in a given industry, whether employers or employees. The hope was that if employers and workers in, say, the building industry jointly settled their problems, this would promote social harmony. It was also hoped that, if power could be diffused to strong vocational groups, there would be less need of a strong state.

On looking back, the surprising thing about the Catholic social movement in Ireland was that it did not have more success. It had no ideological competitors. There were practically no communists in Ireland. Even social democrats or liberals in the continental meaning of those terms were rare. The great majority of the population were practising Catholics. One might have thought that a movement appealing to Catholic principles would have been kicking at an open door.

The difficulty with vocational organisation was that it meant breaking up established habits of work in government and civil service. Ireland was a parliamentary democracy on the British model. The civil service was divided into departments, and each department was headed by a minister responsible to the Dáil. This meant that it was difficult to hive off authority to vocational bodies. Who would answer for them to the Dáil? What would happen if they contravened government policy? It was easier for politicians and civil servants to stick to the system they were used to.

The issue had already come to a head before the period covered by this book began. In 1938 the then Taoiseach, Mr de

Valera, had set up a commission to examine how best to bring vocational organisation to Ireland. The commission had reported in 1944, recommending an elaborate structure of interlocking vocational councils. Its proposals had been treated with a freezing lack of interest by Mr de Valera's government. To enthusiasts for the Catholic social movement, this seemed like sinning against the light. Here were Catholic ministers, in a Catholic country, doing nothing to implement a scheme based on Catholic principles. From then on they were on the lookout, awaiting any opportunity to nudge the development of the state in a vocational direction.

This helps to explain the background to the most celebrated Church-State crisis of this period—the mother-and-child-scheme episode of 1951. The young Minister for Health in the first inter-party government, Dr Noel Browne, introduced a scheme to provide free maternity care for all mothers and expectant mothers, and free medical care for all children up to the age of sixteen. Irish infant mortality was high by the standards of neighbouring countries, and the scheme was a determined attempt to raise standards in a field where improvement was needed. But it did entail an extension of state control. The vocationalists were up in arms. They were not the only group opposed to Dr Browne. The Irish Medical Association had its own reasons for opposing the scheme. Dr Browne was already, for reasons unconnected with the scheme, on bad terms with his party leader and colleague in the cabinet, Sean MacBride. Some of his other cabinet colleagues were unhappy at his handling of the matter. But these factors by themselves would probably not have been enough to stop Dr Browne pushing his scheme through. It was the argument from Catholic social teaching that was decisive. For it enabled opponents of the scheme to appeal to the Catholic bishops on a matter of religious principle. The hierarchy decided that the scheme was indeed contrary to Catholic social teaching, and asked the government to withdraw it. Dr Browne's cabinet colleagues refused to support him, he resigned, and the scheme was dropped. A lot more could be said about the mother-and-child-scheme crisis. But its significance, for the purpose of this essay, is that it could only have happened at this moment in Irish history. It was only then that Catholic social principles were sufficiently distinctive, and held with sufficient assurance, for the hierarchy to base a condemnation upon them.

For the mother-and-child scheme was only the most dramatic of a number of episodes, arising out of the application of Catholic social teaching, which occurred during the 1950s. About the time that Dr Browne was framing his mother-and-child scheme, his colleague William Norton, the Minister for Health and Social Welfare, was planning an extension of the state's social insurance scheme. The more ardent vocationalists attacked this as another undue extension of state power. Mr Norton kept on closer terms with the hierarchy than Dr Browne, and his scheme was not condemned. But at the time, it attracted more criticism from enthusiasts for Catholic social teaching than Dr Browne's did. In 1952–3, the Fianna Fáil government had trouble with the hierarchy when it tried to introduce a modified version of Dr Browne's scheme; but by largely symbolic amendments it was able to avert a condemnation. In 1955 James Dillon, Minister for Agriculture in the second inter-party government, proposed to centralise agricultural education in a new state-run Agricultural Institute. The scheme was attacked by, among others, several bishops, who argued that it marked an unwarranted extension of state power, and Mr Dillon had to withdraw it. The Agricultural Institute which was eventually set up is purely a research body.

The atmosphere of the 1960s was very different. Demands for vocational organisation died away. This followed changes in the climate of opinion elsewhere, for the continental Catholics who had developed the vogue for vocationalism were losing interest in it by the end of the 1950s. Suspicion of state power died away too. As the 1960s wore on, government departments were increasingly likely to be criticised for not doing enough, rather than for doing too much. As social research developed it became clear that the Irish state was doing too little for many of its citizens. There were whole groups in society—the aged, the mentally-handicapped, the subsistence farmers of the West, the itinerants—who needed more support. Churchmen did as much as any to make this clear. Some of the best-known social reformers of the 1960s were priests, such as Father James McDyer, who brought self-help to a Donegal parish, or Father Thomas Fehily, a pioneer of work among the itinerants.

As controversy about the state's role died away, controversy about the Church's role developed. The 1960s differed sharply from the 1950s in that the activities of the Church itself became a target for criticism. In private, of course, this had always happened; but it was a new thing for it to be found in the media. The change can be precisely dated, to the end of 1963 or the beginning of 1964. Two events occurred at that time. The first was that two well-known Catholic scholars of liberal views, Father John Courtney Murray from the United States and Father Gregory Baum from Canada, were forbidden to lecture in the diocese of Dublin. This was not the first time that such a thing had happened under the regime of the then archbishop, Dr McQuaid; but what was new was that the fact was reported, and commented on, in the press. The second event was that an émigré journalist, Peter Lennon, published some articles fiercely critical of the Irish Catholic Church in an English newspaper, the *Guardian*. The articles were reprinted in some Irish papers and commented on in others. These two events broke the dam. Inhibitions disappeared, and thereafter the media handled religious affairs with as much freedom as they did secular. The rest of the 1960s saw recurring controversy on religious issues—family planning, the role of the Church in education, the ban on Trinity College, censorship, the enshrining of Catholic values in the constitution.

Not only was the Church more subject to criticism, it was also more ready to change. During the 1960s, the vernacular replaced Latin in the liturgy. Altars were turned round so that the priest faced the people, instead of having his back to them, when he said mass. New forms of catechetics were imported from abroad. Irish Catholic missionaries, already strongly represented in Africa and Asia, extended their work to Latin America. This missionary effort was no longer purely clerical : it was becoming increasingly common for laymen to give a part of their careers to service overseas. At home, the charismatic movement and the ecumenical movement were both developing by the end of the 1960s. Catholic and Protestant scholars were meeting each other with increasing frequency in venues such as Greenhills and Glenstal, and in 1970 the Irish School of Ecumenics, under Father Michael Hurley S.J., was founded at Milltown. In the same year, the Catholic hierarchy made its own contribution to improving relations by removing the historic ban on Catholic students attending Trinity College.

The pace of change was particularly marked in the schools. The Catholic Church in Ireland had a uniquely strong grip on the educational system. Neutral or state schools, such as were found in most countries, did not exist in Ireland. All primary schools were denominational, and the Catholic ones were managed by a parish priest or religious order. Secondary schools received financial aid from the state, but they were privately owned, charged fees, and were mostly provided by religious orders. Only the vocational schools, run by local authorities, were not under Church control.

During the 1960s, the Department of Education began quite suddenly to take a more active role in shaping the education system than it had ever done before. It amalgamated many small rural primary schools. It gave grants to secondary schools for building and development. It encouraged small secondary and vocational schools to co-operate. It set up comprehensive schools in areas where the existing post-primary provision was inadequate. Above all, it put unprecedented fresh demands on the secondary schools by introducing free post-primary education in 1968. Past experience would have led one to expect opposition from the hierarchy to these changes. It had always reacted with extreme suspicion to anything that looked like the slightest encroachment by the state on its control of schools. But with a few local exceptions, this did not happen. The bishops welcomed the increase of state activity in the educational field even though it inevitably meant some reduction in their own authority.

I have painted the 1960s as a period of new openness and flexibility in Irish Catholicism. Why was this so? The basic reason was that the Irish Catholic Church stood at the conjuncture of two tidal waves of change : change in Irish society, and change in the world-wide Catholic Church.

The change in Irish society has been recognised by all commentators. Sometime around the end of the 1950s the country passed a watershed. After years of disappointing performance, the economy suddenly began to grow. With growing prosperity came psychological changes : a new adventurousness and a new self-confidence. These developments inevitably had their effect on the Church. They were one cause of the increasing readiness among churchmen to re-examine old ways of doing things. And the changes in the school system would not have been possible if there had not been more money available.

A result of the new affluence was that the country could afford its own television service. Telefís Éireann began transmission on New Year's Day 1962. One effect of television is that it personalises the news. If a public figure makes a decision, he can no longer get away with a printed hand-out to the press : the television newsmen will expect to interview him. And if they interview him, they will cross-question him. Before long this was happening to bishops. Younger listeners, accustomed to seeing bishops on television, may not realise what an innovation this was. Before the mid-1960s, it was unheard of for an Irish bishop to submit himself to interview. Another effect of television is that it thrives on controversy. A newspaper may get away with a single, slanted presentation for years on end : but a current affairs programme on television soon becomes boring if it does not portray the cut and thrust of contending viewpoints. This applies to religion as much as to anything else. This was perhaps the biggest single reason for the increase in religious controversy during the 1960s. Most of the major controversies of the decade started off with a television programme. Gay Byrne's *Late Late Show* was particularly important here. There was one period in the mid-1960s when it seemed to spark off a new controversy almost every Saturday. Viewers could sit up to hear what new criticism Brian Trevaskis or Conor Cruise O'Brien had to make against the Church; or could open their Sunday papers the following morning to see which bishop had censured the programme.

However, change in Ireland itself would not have had such an effect if it had not coincided with change in the Catholic Church as a whole. The 1960s was the period of John XXIII and the Second Vatican Council, when all sorts of forces in the Church which had hitherto been the preserve of enthusiasts and frowned on by authority suddenly became respectable. One was the movement for liturgical reform. A second was the ecumenical movement. A third was the acceptance of freedom of speech within the Church. During the Second Vatican Council the bishops were visibly split into parties, and their example was followed by clergy and laity. After all, the Council itself encouraged Catholics to speak their minds frankly. The issue which aroused the most passionate discussion was birth control : was the Church's traditional opposition to artificial means of contraception still tenable? Finally, in 1968, Pope Paul VI came down against a change in the rules, but by then it was too late to reimpose uniformity. Many Catholics had taken their own decisions on the matter. If all these changes were to be found in Irish Catholicism, it was because they had first been developed in other parts of the Catholic Church.

The Protestant minority also found this a period of change. The 1950s were not an entirely comfortable time for Protestants. At the personal level, relations were almost everywhere good, and it would be absurd to portray Protestants as living in fear of persecution. But at the public level, episodes occurred which gave them some unease. An organisation called *Maria Duce* campaigned for a change in the constitution which would proclaim the Roman Catholic Church as the one true church. *Maria Duce* was on the lunatic fringe of Irish politics, but it was able to attract crowds of thousands to its rallies. In 1950 the Knights of St Columbanus succeeded, by skilful exploitation of the rules, in wresting the Meath Hospital, a traditionally Protestant establishment, from Protestant control—though it is fair to add that an Act of the Oireachtas soon restored its previous management. In 1957, the Protestants of the village of Fethard-on-Sea in County Wexford suffered a boycott by their Catholic neighbours, because they were believed to have helped the Protestant partner in a mixed marriage to abscond with her children to Northern Ireland. Though Mr de Valera, then serving in his last term as Taoiseach, condemned the boycott, the Catholic bishop and clergy supported it. In 1958 two Protestant preachers at Killaloe, County Clare, were assaulted by local Catholics. The District Justice convicted the assailants, but his comments showed that his sympathies were with them. 'When men come to an Irish village and provoke the people by foisting their views upon them, they are abusing whatever rights they have under the constitution,' he said. To some Protestants, this was evidence that the Catholic majority would not give to the minority the same liberty of speech as they expected for themselves.

The *cause célèbre* of the 1950s was the Tilson judgment.

Protestants had long resented the promise which the Catholic Church exacted from the non-Catholic partner in a mixed marriage that all the children would be brought up as Catholics. Down to 1950, the Irish courts had avoided taking sides in the matter. But in the Tilson case of that year, they had to rule on the upbringing of the children in a mixed marriage which had broken up. They decided that they would take cognisance of the pre-nuptial promise given by the non-Catholic partner. By so doing, the courts seemed to many Protestants to have taken the Catholic side in an issue which caused special bitterness between Protestant and Catholic.

The 1960s, however, saw, for Protestants as well as for Catholics, a change in atmosphere. There were no new Fethards-on-Sea, or repeats of the Tilson judgment. The growth of the ecumenical movement led to a fresh awareness among Catholics of Protestant sensitivities. In every way, the Protestant minority was becoming increasingly integrated. In 1965 a journalist on the *Irish Times*, Michael Viney, asked 'a group of some thirty young Protestants, from all parts of the country, if they felt there was any discrimination known to them which might influence their choice of career'. None of them could think of any.

True, the Protestant segment of the population continued to fall in numbers—by 24 per cent between the census of 1946 and that of 1971. But no one claimed that this was because life was more difficult for Protestants. The Protestant emigration rate was lower than the Catholic during this period. Professor Brendan Walsh, Ireland's leading demographer, has analysed the reasons for the decline. The biggest single reason was that the Catholic birth rate was much higher than the Protestant—by over 60 per cent. The second most important reason was that the Protestant death rate was much higher than the Catholic—a difference of over 50 per cent—caused by the fact that the Protestant population contained a much higher proportion of elderly people. But there was a third factor—the number of Protestants who made mixed marriages, and whose children, therefore, were lost to the Protestant community. There is evidence that the proportion of mixed marriages was increasing during the 1950s and 1960s. This was ironic, for an increase in mixed marriages was a sign of increasing integration. Thus the increasing integration of the Protestant community was a cause of its numerical decline.

The picture I have painted here is one of rapid change. The change took place on a platform of stability. In the formal practice of their religion, the standards of Irish Catholics remained uniquely high. A survey in 1971 showed that 96 per cent of the Catholic population claimed to have attended mass the previous Sunday. True, the number of vocations to the priesthood dropped sharply during the 1960s, but the decline showed signs of levelling out by the end of the decade. Religious observance among the Protestant minority was also unusually high by international standards. But when this is said, the emphasis on change seems deserved. At the beginning of the 1950s, Irish Catholicism appeared monolithic and triumphalist; by the end of the 1960s it was self-questioning, more open-minded, and divided between different opinions. At the beginning of this period, relations between the denominations at the official level were wary and suspicious; by the end they were cordial, and marked by ecumenism. There was a good cause for saying that, during these twenty years, religion in Ireland changed more quickly than in any period of similar length since the Reformation.

Developments in the Irish Legal System since 1945

Bryan M. E. McMahon

Any attempt to discern or identify the major developments that have influenced the Irish Legal System since the end of World War II must deal with four developments in particular. First, since the end of the War, and in particular since the late 1950s, the development and growth of the welfare state. Secondly, the discovery by lawyers in the early 1960s that the 1937 Constitution (Bunreacht na hÉireann) was a legal document which limited government action on the one hand, and guaranteed individual freedoms on the other. Thirdly, the political tensions that erupted in Northern Ireland in 1968, and which have remained with us, more or less continuously, since that date. Fourthly, and finally, regard must be had to Ireland's accession to the European Communities in January 1973.

First, the expansion of the welfare state concept. The changing nature of the role of the state in managing the affairs of the nation has had far-reaching effects in the legal system. In the nineteenth century and the early part of the twentieth century, the state engaged in a policy of absentionism. Under the influence of *laissez-faire* economic philosophy, the state encouraged individuals to seek their own salvation. Under the illusion that all individuals in society were equal, the state abstained from undue interference and indulged in a kind of 'may the best man win' policy. State regulation was kept to a minimum. In the early part of the twentieth century, and most noticeably in the period that succeeded the World War II, this philosophy gave way to that of the welfare state. The state realised that all citizens were not equal, and that some citizens needed greater assistance than others. It was no longer satisfied with a view which cast it as an unconcerned referee in the social contest. It now saw itself also as the official handicapper whose task involved the equalising of the conditions under which various persons in society competed.

It should be said that in its new role the state not only increased welfare payments of one kind or another to the less well-off sections of the community, it also promoted the interests of the weaker sections of the community by passing specific legislation, such as the Landlord and Tenant and Rent Acts, which strengthened and secured the position of the tenant in the law, the Hire-Purchase Acts 1946–1960, which assisted the hirer of goods in his hire-purchase transactions, and, more recently, the various consumer protection measures (The Consumer Information Act 1978 and the Sale of Goods and Supply of Services Bill, 1978, which replaced the Coalition's proposed Consumer Protection Bill 1978), which gave legislative recognition to the economic environment in which the low-income consumer is continuously subjected to advertising pressures and high-powered sales techniques.

Furthermore, the state began to extend its regulatory role and began to demand registration and licences for activities which had heretofore been free from control. Licences are nowadays required, for various public policy reasons, for a host of activities including, to take a random selection, poultry hatcheries[1], hotels and guest houses[2], and the activities conducted by auctioneers[3], house agents[4], employment agencies[5], banks[6], building societies[7], etc.

Again, since 1953, the state has attempted to ensure fair trading in the economy by passing legislation designed to outlaw various restrictive practices and since 1958, and especially since 1972, the government has extensive powers in controlling prices for consumer goods and services.[8]

No statutory controls on incomes have been attempted, however, but it is worth noting that the non-obligatory National Wage Agreements have been reinforced by the government on two occasions since 1973 in the Regulation of Bank Acts 1973–1975[9] which prevented the banks making pay increases in excess of National Wage criteria.

The shift, therefore, from the *laissez-faire* philosophy to the concept of the welfare state has meant that the state has become more evidently willing to initiate legislation to achieve desirable social ends. Nowhere has the switch had more obvious effects than in the area where the state has attempted to regulate the economy. The increasing awareness by post-war governments of their ability to control and direct the economy, and their increasing desire to do so, has led successive Irish governments to adopt various pieces of legislation to achieve desirable economic objectives. These desirable economic and, indeed, social objectives are now normally set out in what are called economic programmes or plans, and the recent establishment by the new Fianna Fáil government of a Minister for Economic Development and Planning is further evidence of the present government's commitment to its new role as the orchestrator of the economy.

It is in this light that various legal developments, such as those just mentioned (licencing legislation, price controls, restrictive practices legislation, consumer legislation, and developments in the wages area) can be viewed.

More interestingly, however, in its efforts to promote its economic objectives as set out in the various economic programmes, the state in recent decades has sought to control social activity by the use of various incentives. The state seemingly has learned, like many a wise parent, that co-operative action may be more readily obtained by inducements rather than by coercion; carrots, rather than nails, have begun to figure more prominently in the state's efforts to move the social donkey. Accordingly, it has had to resort to grants, subsidies, tax concessions and other incentives, to induce a positive response from individuals and businesses to its economic programme. It is asserted that, in its role as regulator of the economy at least, the use of such incentives by the state is as much a legislative function as the negative regulation that characterised the *laissez-faire* era. Our definition of law must therefore be broadened, at least in the sphere of economic law, to accommodate this new phenomenon.

The assumption by the state of the role of regulator of the economy in the welfare state philosophy, has had several repercussions for the legal system, the most important of which are the following.

First, unlike other branches of law, where parliament's role in the rule-making phase tends to be considerable, if not dominant, in the sphere of social welfare legislation and in the general area of economic law parliament's role is a distinctly limited one. Much economic regulation in this area, for example, is executed by ministerial order, and, while parliament has usually control over the parent act, such control is exercised in advance, and more often than not in a general way, without any appreciation of the detailed problems that subsequently arise. The increasing work-load that parliament has inherited as a result of its expanding role in the welfare state necessitates increased delegation of function.

Second, one may say by way of generalisation that, in spite of recent encouraging developments in the courts, the system of legal protection afforded to the individual in his dealings with the state is inadequately developed in this country. There are many important aspects of administrative law barely adverted to by Irish lawyers, and as an academic subject, administrative law is only recently winning for itself a place in university curricula. The absence of any pre-published criteria relating to some state grants, the absolute discretion vested in some officers administering such schemes, the absence of publicity in this decision-making process and the reluctance of the courts to substitute their discretion for that of the administering officer[10] —all tilt the scales, in a dispute between the individual and the state, very much in favour of the state.

Third, and related to the protection of the individual just mentioned is a fundamental change of attitude in our definition of law. Up to the early part of this century the law was primarily concerned with protecting the state, and indicating to this end, what the citizen should not do. Law was primarily a negative regulator. Law as an instrument for promoting the state's economic policy, however, is only occasionally used in this way at all. When the state wants to promote economic objectives, as it has been increasingly willing to do since 1945, it is very reluctant to use law as coercion. It prefers voluntary participation to compulsive response. In other words, law is being used as an incentive. In promoting its regional policy, for example, the state does not say one must open one's factory in an underdeveloped area; it prefers to say that if one opens the factory in an underdeveloped area then more generous state assistance will become available. In promoting its economic policies at least, the state has switched its emphasis from penalties to rewards; there has been a shift from kicks to kisses. Grants, subsidies, tax concessions, etc., all find their place in this new atmosphere of positive stimulation. The significance of this has not been properly studied by lawyers and it is small wonder that the rules protecting the individual, developed as they were in a penalty-conscious era, are inadequate in the new reward-giving context.

The state, therefore, in exercising its expanded functions in the welfare state atmosphere, puts pressure on the traditional legislative institutions, exposes the limitations of existing definitions of law and illustrates how inadequately the individual's position is catered for in the modern reward-giving context.

The second major development that occurred in the legal system during the period under discussion may be described as 'the discovery of the Constitution'. By 'the discovery of the Constitution' I mean, that it was during this period, commencing in the 1960s, that Irish lawyers began to realise for the first time that Bunreacht na hÉireann was a legal document. Up to the early 1960s there were very few attempts by Irish lawyers to study the Constitution as a source of legal rights, and Constitutional arguments were rarely urged upon the courts at all. This attitude to the Constitution was understandable to some extent insofar as the citizens (including the lawyers) of the Irish Free State, and later of the Republic, were more likely to look upon a new Constitution as a document which primarily expressed political and social values rather than as a document which established the legal system and guaranteed fundamental rights to the citizens.

One is not asserting here, of course, that lawyers were not aware of the Constitution before 1960, but what is suggested is that they did not appreciate the legal possibilities of the Constitution, with the confidence that is necessary, if such appreciation is to be converted into aggressive action before the courts. This may partly be explained by the fact that, as the Irish legal system was historically linked to, and greatly influenced by, the common law, and since the British influence was predominant, the principal precedents followed by the Irish lawyers were those handed down by the Court of Appeal and the House of Lords in England. England did not have a written Constitution, however, in the sense of having a single document comparable to Bunreacht na hÉireann, and, therefore, there were no precedents from that source which might have inspired Irish lawyers. Moreover, the features of British constitutional law, namely, the absence of recognised fundamental rights provisions, the absence of judicial review, and the theory of the absolute sovereignty of Parliament, did not find favour in Bunreacht na hÉireann, and made the search for English parallels in the area of constitutional law futile. No constitutional inspiration could, therefore, be got from the traditional source, and in the absence of such inspiration, it is not surprising that Irish lawyers were somewhat slow to realise the full legal possibilities of the Constitution.

By the mid-1960s, however, things began to change. The standards of legal education began to rise, full-time legal academics became a recognisable force and postgraduate legal studies increased. Many students went to further their studies in law schools in the United States of America, where they recognised that the constitutional parallels between the United States and Ireland were much more relevant than any precedents which might have been found in England. Practising lawyers as well as judges came to realise the importance of the American experience and began to develop and expound Bunreacht na hÉireann.

One successful constitutional action generated others, so that nowadays we have reached the situation in Ireland that a week rarely passes in which constitutional issues are not being argued before the higher courts of the land. Many of these cases deal with fundamental rights provisions of the Constitution, and may be related to the increasing awareness of the sacredness of the citizen's human rights in western society, since the end of the last war. One need only mention the Nuremberg Trials, the Council of Europe's Convention of Human Rights and the United Nations' Declaration of Human Rights, to underline the international parallels.

The increase in constitutional litigation may owe something to the emergence in the 1960s of more articulate and more aggressive minority groups which were prepared to argue their groups' interests at a more fundamental and basic level. Again, the American experience was seminal. One only has to recall the international appeal of Ralph Nader's consumerism, the plaintive Joan Baez singing 'We Shall Overcome', or the moving plea for black equality by Martin Luther King in his letter from Alabama Gaol, to realise the impact of American events in our own country. Minority groups in Ireland began to take courage from the international link-up, and one need only refer to the emergence of consumer associations, environmental groups and feminist organisations (to mention but a few such groups) which were prepared to aggressively assert new social interests in a constitutional context.

The increase in the number of constitutional cases taken in Ireland during the period 1960 to 1967 is a phenomenon that has been noted by Professor J. Kelly in the Foreword to the second edition of his book, *Fundamental Rights in the Irish Constitution* (1967). On page vii he makes the following statement :

'In the six years which have elapsed since the first edition of this book appeared the Irish Courts have pronounced decisions in constitutional cases which rival, in number and in weight, those of the whole preceding period since the Constitution was enacted in 1967; and as these pages went to press, some further important cases were pending. Both Bench and Bar are increasingly tending to fertilise Irish jurisprudence by implanting in it concrete propositions evolved from fundamental principles, and the rate of development over the next few years is likely to be rapid, particularly, perhaps in the areas of "access to the Courts" and of the undefined personal rights guaranteed by Article 40.3.1.'

Professor Kelly's prediction has been more than borne out in the decade 1967–77.

What then, in specific terms, was the result of this new awareness? The increased judicial activity generated by these events saw several new and important constitutional principles established. The Supreme Court has held, for example, that it is not strictly bound by its own previous decisions,[11] thereby departing from the strict rule of *stare decisis* which operates elsewhere in the system. In the case of *Byrne v. Ireland*[12] the theory of state immunity, which sprung from the British Constitutional theory that 'The King can do no wrong', was abandoned. In *Ryan v. The Attorney-General*[13] in 1965, Mr Justice Kenny held that as well as the personal rights specifically mentioned in Article

D

40 of the Constitution, there also exists a number of unspecified rights, and these unspecified rights have been occupying the courts ever since. The courts have by now, with what one commentator termed as startling speed,[14] more or less recognised that the following additional rights are guaranteed by the Constitution although not specifically mentioned therein : the right to bodily integrity,[15] the right to dispose of, and withdraw, one's labour, the right not to join a union,[16] the right to earn one's livelihood,[17] the right to work,[18] the right to litigate,[19] the right to prepare for and follow a chosen career,[20] the right to consult and be represented by a lawyer,[21] the right to marry,[22] the right to marital privacy[23] and the right to free movement within the State.[24]

Furthermore, a refusal to grant an arrested person access to a legal adviser has been held to be an infringement of a constitutional right, and statements taken from such persons have been held to be inadmissible as evidence.[25] Moreover, it has now been held that the individual whose constitutional rights have been infringed can in the appropriate circumstances bring an action for damages for such a breach of right, even though there was no conventional heading at common law under which he might sue.[26]

All this represents an exciting development in which the Constitution is being explored, is being explained and is being continuously examined by lawyers and judges alike.

The third major development that has occurred in the Irish legal system during this period must be directly attributed to the political disturbances that have erupted in this island since 1968. These events have impinged upon the legal system in many ways. They have been directly responsible for the Fifth Constitutional Amendment, which removed from the Constitution the express reference to the Catholic Church; for the establishment by proclamation of the Special Criminal Court on 26 May 1972 which dispenses with the right to trial by jury; for the passing of the Criminal Injuries Act 1970, the Criminal Law Act 1976, the Criminal Law (Jurisdiction) Act 1976 and the Emergency Powers Act 1976 (this last, when referred to the Supreme Court by President Ó Dálaigh, was the cause of another constitutional crisis). The courts, too, became occupied with issues which arose directly out of the political situation :

former ministers were prosecuted for alleged criminal activities; the constitutionality of several government measures were contested before the courts; as well as President Ó Dálaigh's reference, already mentioned, Kevin Boland unsuccessfully contested the constitutionality of the Sunningdale Agreement.[27] Furthermore, the courts were called on to define the rights of persons held on seven-day detention orders, especially in relation to access to medical and legal assistance.[28]

The allegations of police brutality also stimulated some criminal prosecutions and some civil actions, and finally caused a formal enquiry to be made under the chairmanship of Mr Justice Barra Ó Briain.[29]

Moreover, as a result of allegations against the British government of brutality used by the security forces in Northern Ireland. the Irish government successfully prosecuted the United Kingdom in Strasbourg for breach of the Council of Europe's Convention on Human Rights.

The political disturbances, therefore, had repercussions in the Constitution itself, in legislation and in the decisions of the national and international courts, and they called for legal response, not only from the executive branch of government, but from the legislators, from the judiciary and, in the case of the constitutional amendment, from the people itself.

Extensive as these visible repercussions were on the legal system, they must represent only in a very small way the negative effect that the political disturbances had on the legal system. (These disturbances of course, one must remember included the burning of the British Embassy and the assassination of the British Ambassador.) The hours spent by the Cabinet, by civil servants, by Gardai Siochana in security-related discussions were, presumably, at the expense of other worthwhile tasks in the legislation and enforcement areas.

The picture can be described in the following way : the legitimate government, feeling threatened by destructive forces within the state, felt justified in resorting to repressive legislation. There were counterforces, however, operating against such legislation. In the early years, at any rate, say from 1968 to 1973, the Irish public had shown certain equivocation towards what the governments of the day described as 'subversives'. One has to call to mind the events of Bloody Sunday, the Widgery Report and the Compton and Parker Reports on brutality and methods on interrogation to appreciate this equivocation.

Moreover, some civil rights groups and some liberals were quick to point out the dangers of such repressive legislation, and resort was had once more to the courts to adjudicate on the constitutionality of the legislative measures and to more clearly define the limits of such legislation : the state's legislative reaction to the subversives provoked a counter-reaction from defence lawyers and civil liberties groups which sometimes ended in the courts. Ironically, therefore, the political disturbances provided the courts with an opportunity which they might otherwise not have had to define clearly what prisoners' rights were in these circumstances. One might say, therefore, by way of metaphor that the social pendulum, which moves in a restricted arc during a period of social stability, began to oscillate in a more lively fashion during the period of political disturbance. In legal terms, the increased pull to the right, as manifest in the various repressive measures, was countered by an equally strong swing to the left, wherein the courts were asked to define the limits of the state's rights in these circumstances. One may say that while supporters of individual liberties saw their freedoms being eroded by state legislative measures, this very same legislation provoked the liberals to contest the legislation before the courts, thereby providing the courts, in the end, with an opportunity of better defining the vague fundamental rights guaranteed in the Constitution.

The final development which must be noted even in this short review is of more recent origin, and was caused seemingly by external economic developments, especially on the continent of Europe. I refer, of course, to the Common Market. In May 1972, the Irish people in the Third Amendment to the Constitution overwhelmingly voted to join the European Economic Community. The statutory legislation required to give effect to these decisions was enacted in the European Communities Act 1972 and was subsequently amended in 1973 and 1977. This legislation recognised the enormous significance that accession to the European Community would have for Ireland. It, in effect, made the Establishing Treaties, all the Regulations, the Directives and the Decisions of the Community, part of our domestic law and gave rights to individuals which the national courts were obliged to uphold. The legislation also established a Joint Committee of the Oireachtas to act as a watch-dog for the legislation which was necessitated by our membership.[30] One does not have the space to spell out even in a general way the full implications which this had for Ireland, but suffice to say that, in the sphere of economic law at least, the consequences were all-pervasive. The business community had new rights, and where Community law and Irish legislation conflicted the former was to prevail. Irish judges and lawyers had now to familiarise themselves with the whole corpus of Community law, and if in doubt as to what Community law was on any particular topic the Irish courts could refer (and in some cases were indeed obliged to refer) the matter for authoritative interpretation to the Court of Justice of the European Communities in Luxembourg. When one realises that the Treaty of Rome alone covers the free movement of goods, of persons, of services and of capital, and extends to all areas of economic activity, including agriculture and fisheries, one begins to see the vast implications for the Irish legal system. A few statistics will help to substantiate this claim. In the five-year period January 1973 to December 1977 a total of ten acts of parliament were passed by the Oireachtas and 108 ministerial regulations were issued under authority contained in the European Communities Act 1972. Moreover, a further twenty-nine statutory instruments necessitated by membership were issued under legislation other than the European Communities Act 1972. This legislation covered such disparate matters as harmonisation measures relating to food standards in sugar (S.I. No. 118 of 1975), regulations relating to road passenger transport (S.I. No. 388 of 1977), recognition of medical qualifications (S.I. No. 288 of 1976), schemes for the retirement of farmers (S.I. No. 163 of 1976), requirements relating to minimum stocks of petroleum oils (S.I. No. 59 of 1976) and measures which declared false testimony before the European Court of Justice to be perjury (Court of Justice of the European Communities (Perjury) Act 1975).

On the judicial front, too, the impact of membership has become noticeable. Several references have been made to the Court of Justice under Article 177 of the Treaty of Rome (e.g. *North Kerry Milk Products Ltd v. The Minister for Agriculture and Fisheries*, Case 80/76, 22 March 1976; *Bord Bainne v.*

Minister for Agriculture, Case 92/77, 23 February 1978; *Minister for Fisheries v. Schonenberg, et al*, Case 88/77) and there have been instances where the national courts have taken cognisance of the supremacy of Community legislation over national laws (*Minister for Fisheries v. Peter Stam*, Cobh District Court, 2 December 1977, Unreported). Moreover, although not readily quantifiable, EEC law has undoubtedly been a noticeable factor in commercial and legal negotiations, in changes in commercial practices (especially because of Articles 85 and 86 of the Treaty of Rome) and in out-of-court settle- ments.[31] More and more, our legislation is being formulated in Brussels; more and more, our lobbying and our input to such a legislative process must be made in Europe. Extensive as the European dimension is, however, one must not exaggerate its influence. There are still many areas of law which remain un- affected by Community legislation. The Irish lawyer, however, has to familiarise himself with Community law, not only to discharge his professional duties in the areas affected, but also to enable him to act with confidence in those areas which remain unaffected.

The above developments show in some measure how the legal system was influenced by internal and external, social, economic and political events during the period 1945–1977. In so far as the external influences are concerned it may be worth noting that these no longer predominantly come from England. The Irish legal system is increasingly being influenced by events and developments occurring in Europe and the United States of America.

NOTES

1. Poultry Hatcheries Act 1947 (No. 49 of 1967).
2. Tourist Traffic Act 1939 (No. 24 of 1939) and Tourist Traffic Act 1957 (No. 27 of 1957).
3. Auctioneers and House Agents Act 1947–1973 (No. 10 of 1947 and No. 23 of 1973).
4. *Ibid.*
5. The Employment Agency Act 1971 (No. 27 of 1971).
6. The Central Bank Act 1971 (No. 24 of 1971).
7. The Building Societies Act 1976 (No. 38 of 1976).
8. The Prices Act, 1958 (No. 4 of 1958) amended by the Prices

(Amendment) Acts, 1965 and 1972 (No. 23 of 1965 and No. 20 of 1972).

9. Regulation of Banks (Remuneration and Conditions of Employment) (Temporary Provisions) Acts 1973 and 1975 (Nos. 12 of 1973 and 27 of 1975). Minister exercised statutory powers to freeze bank salaries in SI No. 196 of 1973 and SI No. 305 of 1975. See also Act No. 18 of 1976.

10. See *Corporation of Limerick v. Sheridan* 90 ILTR 59; *Central Dublin Development Association Ltd & Others v. A.G.* 109 ILTR 85; *Kiely v. Minister for Social Welfare* (1971) IR 21.

11. *Attorney General v. Ryan's Car Hire Ltd* (1965) IR 642.

12. (1972) IR 241.

13. (1965) IR 294.

14. Heuston, 'Personal Rights Under the Irish Constitution 1976', The Irish Jurist 205 at 221.

15. *Ryan v. Attorney-General* supra. footnote 13.

16. *Educational Co. of Ireland v. Fitzpatrick* (1961) IR 345.

17. *Murtagh Properties Ltd v. Cleary* (1972) IR 330.

18. *Murphy v. Stewart* (1973) IR 97.

19. *Murtagh Properties Ltd v. Cleary* (1972) IR 330.

20. See *Landers v. Attorney-General* (1975) 109 ILTRI.

21. *The State (Healy) v. Donoghue* (1976) IR 325.

22. See *Ryan v. Attorney-General*, supra. footnote 13.

23. *McGee v. Attorney-General*, (1973) IR 284.

24. See *Ryan v. Attorney-General*, supra. See also *The State (K.M. and R.D.) v. Minister for Foreign Affairs, M. Burke Passport Officer and Attorney-General* H.Ct. 29 May 1978. Unreported.

25. *The People (DPP) v. Madden.* See Heuston, supra. footnote 14, generally.

26. *Mescell v. CIE* (1973) IR 121.

27. (1974) IR 338.

28. See Heuston, supra. footnote 14, at 221.

29. Report of the Committee to recommend certain safeguards for persons in custody and for members of An Garda Siochana, PRL 7158. Presented to the government on 13 April 1978.

30. See generally for effect of this legislation McMahon, I Eur. Law Rev. 86–90 and 2 Eur. Law Rev. 150–154.

31. *Sugar Distributors Ltd. and Thomas Keleghan v. Cómhlucht Siúcre Eireann Teoranta* (High Court, May 1975). Noted McMahon, 2 Eur. Law Rev. 153–154.

The Environment, 1945-70

Brendan Clarke

Any study of the physical environment is concerned with both human and scientific analysis. It is no one's preserve. It is the limitless pursuit of academic disciplines. Architects, engineers, economists, sociologists and naturalists, can all make their contributions to the fertilisation of this vast subjective expanse. 'We must remind ourselves,' says John Kenneth Galbraith, 'that specialisation is a scientific convenience, not a scientific virtue.' It is my first conclusion, therefore, that above all else, the environment is the stomping ground of the ordinary man. The desires and ambitions of the politician, the artisan and the backwoodsman are entitled to respect.

Where the environment begins and where it ends, has never been and never will be defined. It is an area of interest bounded only by the cosmos. It is everyone's interest and no one's in particular. It is deeply personal and yet so obviously universal. No element in political economy is so elusive of satisfactory administrative response.

I have decided to confine this essay to an historical commentary on the legislation and institutional framework which was most directly concerned with the Irish environment in the post-war period, with some reference to earlier foundations and broader perspectives. Thus manacled, I shall leave the political and technological evaluations to others more professionally fitted than I.

Concern for the physical environment in which we live is heightened by the pressures of urbanisation, industrialisation and population growth. Small wonder then that the physical environment did not become a burning political issue in the entire history of the Irish Free State.

The debate on the 'Treaty', which formally began at Christmastime in 1921, was not to ease for the next 40 years. It was the over-riding political preoccupation. Whatever residue of social energy remained was spent, first in a bitter civil war, then upon efforts to overcome the vicissitudes of economic depression. The economic war with Britain, high protectionism, a brief flirtation with European fascism and the miseries of the emergency during the world war, added to the dissipation of national creativity. Throughout that period unemployment and emigration were the apocalyptic twins threatening the viability of the state itself.

A society with a small, heavily rural population and high unemployment was hardly going to become heated about a physical environment upon which the demographic pressures were easing rather than increasing, and in which industrial and infrastructural expansion were hardly noticeable. In the slumbering 1930s and 1940s the motor car was posing little threat; nor did pollution of the air, water and rural amenities aggravate the anxieties of public representatives. True there was concern over the decay of the rural village and the increasing decrepitude of the inner city.

In the 1930s there were four items of conservation legislation —the National Monuments Act, the Game Preservation Act, the Forestry Acts and the Wild Birds Protection Act.

It was the last of these which contained a clause setting apart the North Bull island at Dollymount as the first official bird sanctuary.

Before 1930 there had been no bird sanctuary in Ireland. Nesting birds had been protected for many years on Lambay Island and on the Skelligs, but there was no official sanctuary of the kind which was common in Britain and on the Continent. When the Wild Birds Protection Bill was being drafted, Father P. G. Kennedy, SJ and Senator S. Brown, SC succeeded in having a clause inserted which made it legally possible to have bird sanctuaries in the Free State. The North Bull island was chosen as a sanctuary because it combined a degree of seclusion for the wild birds and access to interested students. Since Watters had written his Natural History of Ireland in 1853, it had commanded honourable mention in many studies and commentaries. No less than 130 different species of bird had been observed on the island and there was an abundant food supply. Above all, it was argued, proximity to Dublin provided a rare educational facility for universities and schools.

The North Bull sanctuary had prospered for only a few years when early in May 1944 the Golf Clubs were informed that the Irish Tourist Board had taken control of the island and was preparing plans for its development as a tourist resort. The Royal Dublin Club was informed that an amusement park would be sited at the clubhouse. The Irish Society for the Protection of Birds took fright and made immediate enquiries as to the future plans of the Tourist Board. No reply was received but the newspapers began to turn out stories about a veritable honky-tonk paradise with cinema, dancehall, restaurant and lido on the lines of Blackpool. At last at the end of 1945 maps were published showing these torrid features and indicating a bus route running down half the length of the island, with another dancehall at the far end among the dunes.

'It is proposed to let sites for the development of private enterprise' said *The Irish Independent* on 4 November. A year later, on 7 November 1946, *The Irish Times* noted: 'The City Manager's proposals provide for an embankment and bridge linking the island with the mainland at the Dollymount end; the development of 86 acres of the Bull Wall end of the island, which would include the provision of restaurants, dance-hall, an open air theatre, amusement park and various other amenities, and the construction of a road along the north front of the Bull Island for vehicular traffic and for convenient access to various parts of the island at present inaccessible.'

It was clear that the main resting and feeding grounds would be built on or destroyed by the activities of developers and visitors.

In the March 1949 issue of *Studies*, Father P. G. Kennedy, SJ made an impassioned plea for the survival of the sanctuary in the teeth of this popular 'Blue Lagoon Scheme'. It is interesting to note that he suggested Sandymount Strand as a far more suitable area for these playground activities and quoted a consulting engineer who writing in the March 1935 issue of *Studies* had proposed a development from the Pigeon House to Blackrock including an aerodrome, marine lake, playground, amusements park and housing estate.

In *At the Sign of the Three Candles*, 1953, Father Kennedy

reported with a sigh of relief that the 'cold war' against the sanctuary, having continued relentlessly until 1950 was suddenly ended when it was mentioned at a meeting of the Town Planning Committee of Dublin Corporation that the Irish Tourist Board had withdrawn from the 'Blue Lagoon Scheme'. The sanctuary had been spared.

This was a unique incident. There was no national conservation programme at that time. The term 'physical environment' had yet to be imported from the greyer, burgeoning economies of post-war Europe and America.

In the absence of comprehensive legislation, piecemeal measures, scattered and incohesive gave modest witness to the quiet anticipation of the public representative. The Arterial Drainage Act of 1940 and the Turf Development Acts did impinge on the ecology of the countryside, but they did not elicit any strong criticism until the 1960s. The Rivers Pollution Prevention Acts of 1876 and 1893 had been transmitted from British times. They contained the principal powers of Irish local authorities to control water pollution from before the turn of the century. Together with the early Public Health Acts they were, however, to prove largely ineffective when the rapid industrial growth during the First Programme for Economic Expansion surprised the nation. Indeed, while the Water Supplies Act of 1942 and the Fisheries (Consolidation) Act of 1957, were to become useful mechanisms in their time, it is only now with the passing of the recent Water Pollution Act that we realise the inadequacy of these measures.

The isolated Alkali etc., Works Regulation Act of 1906, which required alkali, cement and smelting works to control emissions of noxious and offensive gases, had a useful function in the early part of the century, but by the end of the World War II it was no longer adequate. In 1957 the Department of Local Government in co-operation with certain industrial and other bodies, initiated air pollution measures and in 1970 the Control of Atmospheric Pollution Regulations were made, in an attempt to check the more immediately objectionable types of air pollution. An important development in 1952 was the Tourist Traffic Act which gave Bord Fáilte powers to protect and maintain historic buildings, sites, shrines and places of scenic, historic, scientific and other interest. This was augmented by another

National Monuments Act 1954. The main environmental legislation of the meagre 1950s was rounded off by the first Oil
Pollution of the Sea Act.

In 1959 the National Soil Survey was established by the
Agricultural Institute to assess the soil resources of the country.
A decade later a detailed soils inventory had been assembled,
providing an invaluable input into the develoment of land-use
studies.

Included in the legislative programme of the 1960s were a
second Oil Pollution Act, two Road Traffic Acts and the Local
Government (Sanitary Services) Act. The list had become formidable. But an encapsulating legislative framework was necessary
to which this amorphous compendium could be related.

If we study the post-war years it soon becomes clear that the
protection of the physical environment as an important public
issue did not begin to gather real momentum until the period
covering the first two national economic plans between 1958 and
1969. This is a useful period for discussion, beginning with the
government's First Programme for Economic Expansion and
the publication of T. K. Whitaker's blue book 'Economic
Development', and closing with the rather exhausted demise
of the Second Programme and the publication of the controversial document, Regional Studies in Ireland, more popularly
referred to as the Buchanan Report.

It is a matter of significance that a formulation of an outline
policy on physical planning did not appear in the First Programme in 1958. Sean Lemass and Kenneth Whitaker probably
reasoned that such an approach would have created a solution
in search of a cause. An industrial upsurge would first have to
stimulate the appropriate response as the environment began
to show the marks of unbalanced development. That instinct
was correct. The pace of industrial development in the next
five years was sufficiently rapid to command quite serious attention to the business of planning the physical environment in
harmony with economic expansion.

The public capital investment projections were dramatically
exceeded. The total increase in Gross National Product over five
years was 23 per cent as against the 11 per cent target. All the
running had been made in the industrial sector. Industrial output
in 1963 was 47 per cent greater than in 1957. Quite unexpectedly

the greatest thrust had come from manufacturing industry.

For the first time in Ireland the politicians could see that rapid development on these dimensions could become a long-term threat to the environment, if protective control with strong legislative teeth was not introduced. In 1962, Neil Blaney, TD, Minister for Local Government, introduced the focal planning legislation. The Local Government (Planning and Development) Bill gave rise to a long concentrated debate in the Dáil and the Seanad. To understand the meaning of this central measure, it is necessary to remember the vacuum which had to be filled. Almost thirty years before, in 1934, there had been a Town and Regional Planning Act. It was amended in the year the war broke out, but although it introduced concepts such as planning authorities, planning districts, planning regions, and planning schemes into official parlance, it was, because of its adoptive character, marked by what the Americans would call a high degree of invisibility.

Section 3 of that early measure stated that a planning scheme was 'for the general purpose of securing the orderly and progressive development of a particular area, whether urban or rural, in the best interests of the community and of preserving, improving and extending the amenities of such areas'.

The general purpose of the 1934 Act was 'to make provision for the orderly and progressive development of cities, towns and other areas, whether urban or rural, and to preserve and improve the amenities thereof and for other matters connected therewith'. Laudable objective, indeed, but why were the effects of the Act so anaemic and why in an amended form could it not have stood up to the exigencies of the 1960s?

In 1951 two barristers, John Miley and Frederick C. King, published an explanatory book for lawyers on Town and Regional Planning Law in Ireland. They observed that not a single planning scheme had been brought into force in the fifteen years of the existence of this measure and concluded that the Act was a dead letter, except for certain interim control provisions which they believed were anyhow alien to the general policy of the code.

Their summary was generally correct if not absolutely accurate. In fact, one local authority, Dublin Corporation, did prepare and adopt a plan before the war, but only as a result of legal action requiring it to do so. Also, Abercrombie and Kelly had drawn up an advisory Dublin Sketch Development Plan for the city some years earlier in 1939. The procedures of the 1934 Act were cumbersome but failure was due mainly to the adoptive nature of the provisions. A local authority could prepare a plan and adopt it, but the Act did not impose an obligation to do so. Once a plan was prepared, presented to the Minister and approved by him, it acquired statutory force, and could not be amended. It was therefore safer, however lacking in courage, to let well enough alone and to avoid the possibility of large payments in compensation for planning restrictions.

The case of *Modern Homes (Ireland) Limited v. Dublin City Corporation* also helped to concentrate the minds of the government and local authorities on the need for new planning legislation. The verdict in this case meant that the Corporation was obliged to draw up planning schemes which, according to the thinking of the time, would have little flexibility. They would require confirmation by the Minister of Local Government; and once that confirmation was announced, the schemes would be binding. In the nature of things, the outcome would have meant that a massive compensation bill would have landed on the desk of the Lord Mayor of Dublin. This was an impossible situation.

The long debate in the Oireachtas on the Local Government (Planning and Development) Act, indicated a new understanding of the necessary balance between economic expansion, the provision of jobs and the protection of the natural and built environment. Every local authority was required to prepare a development plan, which was to be a 'statement of aims'. This plan would be accompanied by explanatory maps and would be required to cover four planning aspects—land-use zoning, roads and traffic, urban renewal and the preservation and improvement of amenities. There were other non-obligatory aspects, but plans for rural areas were required to include objectives for new public services and the extension of existing services. The plan would be open for inspection by the public and objections would be heard. Once adopted, it would acquire the force of law and be subject to periodic review which would give the opportunity of revising objectives.

The most significant advance over the English counterpart act was in the democratic recognition of the public interest in private planning applications which had to be advertised in the newspapers. There was, however, criticism of the system whereby appeals directed at the Minister could sometimes appear to succeed or fail for reasons other than an assessment against objective criteria. It has also been observed that, in spite of this valuable legislation, planning in Ireland has not really got beyond the theoretical stage and that official institutions, as well as environmental pressure groups, have succeeded only in producing a convoluted system of negative control mechanisms sacrificing the positive planning process to discreet cases of development control. The emergence of strategic planning is not broadly evident.

Even today a strong lobby for the planning process has not emerged. This shortcoming must, to a great extent be laid at the doors of the pressure groups. The great efforts made in the Department of Local Government in the first few years of the Act were to be buried in a mountain of appeals as the decade came to a close. A great deal of work was generated in the department and in the local authorities by the disastrous paucity of professional planners.

The imposition of these obligations upon local authorities surprised some observers outside the country. How could the planning mechanism be made to work with so few trained planners available in the country? It was reported that since 1945 the number of students who had qualified in the Republic as planners was three or four. In 1962 a campaign had got underway to indoctrinate staff in local authorities in the purposes and procedures of planning, but it was evident that a huge task was required in the education and training of professional planners. In the same year, Bolton Street College of Technology commenced a part-time post-graduate course in town planning as part of the programme if its School of Architecture. A few years later University College Dublin inaugurated a diploma course in town planning. University College Cork also ran a part-time appreciation course based on sixteen lectures. At the same time it was announced that the Graduate School of Engineering Studies in Trinity College was laying plans to establish a full-time post-graduate course in physical planning leading to a Master of Science degree. This last venture did not get off the ground.

In 1965 an Education and Training Committee was requested by the Minister to review the needs and facilities for the education of planners. The committee presented a report on 24 June 1966 which indicated that there were currently only forty-two planners who were qualified members of the Town Planning Institute in the Republic and fifty-one in Northern Ireland. Of the forty-two here, sixteen were employed by local authorities mostly in Dublin, with some in the Department of Local Government. There was an immediate need for 129 planners and a longer-term need for 183, not including consultants. Central and local government would need about twenty-five new planners each year. However, one must conclude that for the remainder of that decade, education for planners at third level did not get the support that was anticipated. The status of planners, especially non-engineers in local authorities, was suspect; career prospects were ill-defined, and the debate on course content and whether programmes should be pitched at undergraduate or post-graduate levels, or both, was not satisfactorily concluded.

In April 1971, Professor Brenikov of the Department of Town and Country Planning, University of Newcastle-upon-Tyne, speaking in Dublin on this subject said that the main problem was not so much finance as the availability of suitable skilled planners as teachers. Planning teachers required good field experience, but these were the people most prized by the local authorities.

The Second Programme for Economic Expansion published in July 1964 was explicit in its approach to physical planning. The government's comprehensive proposals for physical planning and development would lay particular stress on the provision of adequate capital infrastructure for industrial expansion and on improving basic facilities in rural areas. In exercising their powers and duties in relation to the preservation of amenities in cities, towns and countryside, planning authorities would aim at safeguarding areas of natural beauty and recreational value and at conserving buildings and features of historical and scientific interest.

In 1960 and 1961 the government had requested the United Nations to carry out two expert missions, one on physical planning and one on housing and to advise on the needs and possibilities in these matters. The report of these two teams of experts confirmed the government in its view that there was an urgent need for research, training and development in these areas.

As the Second Programme was published a new institute was being set up which for the first five years would be operated in partnership with the United Nations Special Fund and with the operational assistance of several United Nations experts. An Foras Forbartha, The National Institute for Physical Planning and Construction Research, would as the Minister stated on the appointment of the first board, undertake research into and provide training in and advance knowledge of the physical planning and development of cities, towns and rural areas. It would concern itself with building construction and roads construction including ancillary and related services, installations and equipment. Its activities would also range across environmental services; traffic and transportation; natural features and amenities; and the effects and requirements of economic and industrial, agricultural, commercial, social, demographic, cultural and other changes on all these. This work would be carried out in two divisions, one concerned with planning and conservation and the other with construction. In 1966 division of roads was appended to investigate traffic, road construction and road accidents and in 1969 a division of water resources was added to survey national water resources as well as water pollution.

Mr Blaney pointed out that the institute was unique, 'The research arm of planning is concerned with the complete planning spectrum.'

The first Chairman of the new organisation, G. A. Meagher, noted: 'It deals . . . with the entire physical environment. It is, it seems, unique in this respect in the world.'

What remains unique about An Foras Forbartha to the present day is that it caters in its programme of research and advice for all the main facets of the physical environment—planning, roads, the construction industry, water resources and the natural environment. In other countries these areas of endeavour are usually split between a host of separate agencies set up at different times and often disintegrated in their approach to closely related problems.

Several priority areas of activity were outlined for the institute.

These included on the physical planning side the preparation of specimen plans, county and urban, for the guidance of local authorities; the preparation of a draft development plan for the growth and improvement of the country town; work in the area of balanced regional development with particular reference to the methods of identifying and developing centres of growth and with a view to the institute's active participation in regional planning and research on the technical, financial and organisational aspects of urban renewal; training and education in all these areas.

On the building and construction side, the programme would include the preparation of a national regulatory framework for all building work; the development of practical proposals for the introduction of dimensional co-ordination; a technical evaluation of the design/cost relationship in rural housing; the improvement of site methods and organisation including cost analysis; an economic analysis of the industry in the context of the Second Economic Programme and training and education in all these fields. The institute was also requested to look at nature conservation and amenity development. In 1966 a division of roads was appended to investigate traffic, road construction and road accidents and in 1969 a division of water resources was set up to survey national water resources as well as water pollution. A survey of sixty rivers was immediately instituted with 500 sampling stations. They would be surveyed for quality, volume and potential domestic, industrial, fishing, and amenity use, as well as for taking effluent discharges. Areas of serious pollution would be identified so that the appropriate authorities could initiate remedial measures.

Other bodies were involved with the physical environment. Bord Fáilte, in particular, expanded its work on the protection of historical buildings and places of scenic and scientific interest. The Agricultural Institute was monitoring pollution associated with farm wastes and carrying out research on the possible effects of pesticide and insecticide residues. The Institute for Industrial Research and Standards was concerning itself with problems of effluent discharge standards for industry. The programme of the Department of Lands in forestry development and wildlife conservation was visibly apparent across our landscapes, and the work of the Inland Fisheries Trust had become a noticeable feature on the environmental scene. The Office of Public Works was working away quietly in arterial drainage, inland navigation and the maintenance of increasingly valuable state properties.

An Taisce, modelled on the National Trust in Britain, was founded in 1948. A voluntary pressure group dedicated to the cause of conservation, it became under its first president, the distinguished botanist, Robert Lloyd Praeger, a focus for public education and propaganda. Until the 1960s its work was mostly confined to buildings. Then it directed its attentions to nature conservation. It became a prescribed body under the 1963 Planning and Development Act. Between 1964 and 1967 its membership increased from 300 to 1,200.

A more specialist group, the Irish Georgian Society, dedicated to preserving the heritage of good Georgian architecture was founded in 1958. In its first ten years membership increased to 4,000. It published a quarterly bulletin which promoted eighteenth-century art and architecture and gave running commentaries on restoration projects and conservation battles. Among its early restoration projects was the work on the Francini Room at Riverstown House, County Cork and on the Dromana Gateway in County Waterford. Under its chairman and guiding spirit, Desmond Guinness, it co-operated with the Old Dublin Society, An Taisce and the Wolfe Tone and Robert Emmet Societies on the restoration of Tailor's Hall in Dublin.

Support for these groups was probably due to the excitement generated by several major conservation issues. The demolition of buildings on St Stephen's Green created no less a nervous reaction than the erection by the Electricity Supply Board of a new headquarters at Fitzwilliam Street, one of the great Georgian streetscapes. There was widespread criticism of threats to the survival of the Grand Canal, to the erection of hotels at Killarney's lakes and beside the Rock of Cashel, the construction of the oil terminal in Bantry Bay and the Dublin Port and Docks industrial plans for Sandymount Strand.

The allegedly exclusive social backgrounds of the leadership of some of the new conservation groups, especially the Irish Georgian Society, which established its headquarters in the magnificence of Castletown House, gave rise to jibes that conservation was becoming the preserve of the 'belted earls'. Indeed, this phrase was openly used in one notable controversy by the responsible minister at the time.

Another pressure movement, based on the leftwing thrust of Sinn Fein, directed its energy to campaigns for public ownership of beaches and inland waterways. Their housing action campaign in Dublin was supported by other left-wing groups. The collapse of old tenement houses in the city, notably in Fenian Street (resulting in mortal tragedy) stimulated a new campaign for inner-city rehabilitation. In the early 1960s journalists were writing about such hovels as Keogh Square and the Marshalsea Barracks. Other less well-known but similar centres of destitution provided ammunition for the indignant protesters. In an effort to take the pressure out of the Dublin housing emergency, the Minister and the local authorities began to turn their attentions to the spaces at the foot of the South Dublin hills and to the erection of high rise accommodation at Ballymun. Both the ensuing developments were to attract vociferous criticism in later years.

While it was left to the public representatives to face the invective of the pressure groups, a new generation of professional planners produced a number of strategic plans, all of which were keenly and sometimes hotly debated.

In Dublin the traffic consultant, Professor Schaechterle, submitted a prognosis of traffic. His study technique was to be used internationally by traffic experts but his findings gave rise to fears for the future of the Grand Canal which he suggested should be covered in. Dublin Corporation appointed Dr Nathaniel Lichfield to draw up development proposals for seventy-seven acres of the inner city and Lord Llewlyn Davis and Partners were appointed to advise on the environmental aspects of the Development Plan prepared by Michael O'Brien. Professor Myles Wright was drafted in by the Department of Local Government to advise on the regional aspects of planning in the Dublin area and produced a strategy which would cost £1,000 million by 1985. At the same time, Lichfield was given a similar job in the Limerick region. In 1959 Brendan O'Regan had persuaded Sean Lemass to support the novel Irish concept of a free airport. A new town began to emerge in the wilderness of South Clare under the aegis of an energetic Shannon Free Airport Development Company.

An Foras Forbartha published several early plans. These included a provisional plan for the Galway region by a young American planning advisor, Alan Kreditor, a study of County Donegal by Michael Dower, a provisional plan for Galway City by Gerald Walker and James Eustace and a greenfield site project in New Ross by Geoffrey Copcutt. The Agricultural Institute also published extensive resource surveys of West Cork and West Donegal.

In October 1966 Colin Buchanan and Partners were commissioned by the United Nations in response to a request by the Irish government to carry out regional studies in Ireland. The work was undertaken in association with staff in An Foras Forbartha and Economic Consultants Ltd and the Buchanan Report was published towards the end of 1968. Among the recommendations in this controversial document was a suggestion that the nation's ability to compete in Europe would require a national plan based on three tiers of growth. The main centres of growth would be Cork, Limerick-Shannon and Dublin. A second tier of development was proposed for Waterford, Dundalk, Drogheda, Galway, Sligo and Athlone, based on industrial development in some cases, and on tourism and what was called 'the regional function' in others. In areas such as Counties Kerry, Mayo, Donegal, and a group consisting of Counties Longford, Cavan and Monaghan, a third tier of local growth would be selected to provide public services and focal points for private development.

The Buchanan Report was the subject of much misinterpretation and extraordinary political vituperation which fostered unfounded fears in outlying areas. In retrospect the reaction of some leaders of public opinion was surprising. The growth centre in a regional context had been officially propagated since the late 1950s. It is a pity that many commentators read only the 40-page abridged version of Buchanan, or potted newspaper accounts. In the event, the author returned home and his co-workers were reassigned. As the debate petered out, organisations such as the Industrial Development Authority took the initiative with their own regional policy documents.

But there is more to the environment than scientific inquiry, planning and legislation. 'One test of sound social analysis,' says Galbraith, 'is that it explains small matters as well as great.'

In the post-war years small churches with a new functional design began to appear in the countryside at Ennistymon, Killyon, Rosguill and Drimoleague. Then in the wake of Vatican II new interiors and art forms accompanied the liturgical revival. The new functionalism in architecture was evident in such buildings as the Dublin and Shannon air terminals, Busarus, the new Abbey Theatre, the TV centre, University College at Belfield, Liberty Hall, the colleges of technology and the National Garden of Remembrance.

From the streets of the city singing beggars disappeared and so did the horse-drawn cart and the electric tram. More and more the family car replaced the bicycle. Dark limousine colours gave way to fire engine red, canary yellow and french blue. In 1963 the government set up a council for design and Coras Trachtala established design workshops in Kilkenny. There was also an invasion of colours which banished the drab clothes of earlier days. A profusion of hair and limitless variations of style marked the new ascendancy of the teenager. The ubiquitous transistor pervaded the most remote wilderness and the disco replaced the dancehall.

The decade also ushered in cheap overseas travel with rapturous access for the humble citizen to the smarmy delights of the Costa Brava and the Adriatic. Finally, in 1961, with the introduction of a new state television service, young Ireland was indecently exposed to the daily vicissitudes of the universe, the sedentary delights of foil-wrapped entertainment and the uninhibited views of a new liberalism.

1970 was European Conservation Year, marked by public seminars and a re-examination of objectives. The Irish physical and cultural environment had been subjected to a period of concentrated revolution, far more intense than, though undoubtedly related to, the industrial advances with which the era is so commonly associated.

Language, Literature and Culture
in Ireland since the War

Gearóid Ó Tauthaigh

The very scope of this essay should itself suggest that, in the limited space available to me, I cannot hope to offer an exhaustive analysis of Irish artistic endeavour, nor a litany of notable Irish artists, nor yet a study of 'popular culture' in Ireland since the war. When I speak of culture I speak mainly of 'high' culture, of those with fine sensibilities and with the ability to give concrete expression to such sensibilities. This is not as rarified as it may sound. Significant artistic achievement can, and very often does, have an immediate and general social impact. For example, one of the more remarkable aspects of Irish popular culture in the past twenty-five years, the revival in traditional music, although part of a movement in the wider world, and owing much to the work of Ciarán Mac Mathúna and Comhaltas Ceoltóirí Éireann, nevertheless owed an enormous debt also to the individual genius of Seán Ó Riada. Again, educational advances since the sixties have probably raised popular appreciation of and participation in the visual and performing arts, most notably painting and music. Indeed the weight of evidence suggests that the social climate for artistic endeavour has improved considerably in Ireland since the 1950s. The state, acting for the people, has, through its taxation policy, indicated a healthy esteem for the artist in society. If this be no more than a gesture, as has been suggested, it is nonetheless a most positive gesture.[1]

These are general considerations. The bulk of this essay, however, will be devoted to the language issue and to the concerns of Irish literature since the war, though much of what I say of Irish writers and their concerns applies also to those active in the visual and performing arts.

In examining the Irish language question during the past

thirty years one is immediately struck by a mass of paradoxes and contradictions, remarkable even by Irish standards. On the one hand is the undeniable evidence of retreat and despondency, of widespread loss of faith and hope (and at times even of charity) in the stated national aspiration for revival. The most dramatic failure has been the continual (and continuing) contraction of the Gaeltacht, and the linguistic debilitation which has taken place in what remains of it. By 1966 the population of native Irish-speakers had declined to under 70,000 (less than 20 per cent of what it had been at the foundation of the state). Since then the position has deteriorated further. At the present time the most reliable figures available suggest that the population of the authentic Gaeltacht areas (i.e. where Irish is the habitual community language) may be as low as 32,000.[2] Indeed, it is perfectly clear that if present demographic and linguistic trends are not reversed the Gaeltacht as a distinct linguistic community will not survive this century.

It is not too difficult to list some of the factors which have caused this dramatic decline. Emigration ranks high on the list, and the Gaeltacht shared fully in the human haemorrhage of the 1950s. State neglect must be mentioned, or, more charitably, the inadequacy or inappropriateness of such initiatives in economic and social development as the state did undertake. Incredibly, it was not until 1956 that an attempt was made to officially define the geographical extent of the Gaeltacht. This definition was inaccurate when originally made, and has become increasingly and absurdly inaccurate in the last twenty years. The late 1950s also saw the establishment of a semi-state body, Gaeltarra Éireann, with responsibility for economic and social development in the Gaeltacht. In discharging this responsibility the powers and functions of Gaeltarra Éireann have been changed at regular intervals since its establishment. In the absence of integrated social or community planning, economic development, whether public or private, has often meant an inflow of non-Irish-speaking personnel into Gaeltacht areas. The penetration, indeed saturation of the entire country by English language media of information and entertainment has further eroded the language base in the Gaeltacht. The policy of the Catholic Church has been inconsistent, depending almost entirely on the sensitivity of local bishops to the language factor, though here it must be admitted that the last ten years have seen some improvements. The demands of tourism, the vulnerability of small communities to outside influence, and the fall in morale caused by the national failure on the language front, are further factors in the story of Gaeltacht decline.

Yet even here the picture has not been unrelievedly depressing. In the Gaeltacht, as elsewhere in rural Ireland, after the nadir of despair in the 1950s, the 1960s saw the first serious challenge offered to the defeatism and fatalism of a century. A group of articulate young radicals suddenly found its voice and began demanding policies to arrest the dissolution and disappearance of its own community. These Gaeltacht radicals were generally well-educated, and like similar groups in Northern Ireland, were part of the global dynamics of youth politics and civil rights movements of the late 1960s. The new movement brought results. A special Gaeltacht radio service, which had been an idea and an item on the state's revivalist agenda for over forty years, became a reality in 1972. Politicians began to take note of Gaeltacht demands. An expanding network of Gaeltacht co-operatives gave further evidence of the new mood of confidence and self-reliance in the Gaeltacht in recent years. Finally, the last few years have seen a limited public debate on the demand for a special Gaeltacht Authority (Údarás na Gaeltachta).[3] Its advocates have seen this Authority as a welcome innovation in elected community government and administrative devolution. The government is pledged to produce its own scheme for a Gaeltacht Authority within the near future.

The crucial question which must be asked of this new Gaeltacht confidence and resolution is, has it come too late? Time alone will tell. The situation at the present time is critical. Demographically the Gaeltacht is in a perilous state. There are enormous linguistic problems involved in community reconstruction. To avoid extinction the Gaeltacht must expand and grow. At the time of writing it would be dishonest to pretend that the omens are encouraging. Certainly there is little ground for optimism in the state of the language outside the Gaeltacht. Here the years since the war have seen the continuation of what a distinguished Irish-American described in 1963 as 'a declared government policy of restoration' combined with 'an obvious anaemia in its enforcement'.[4] In fact, the signs of the state's failure and of the consequent anxiety of the revivalists were already unmistakably clear by the early 1940s. The revival of the Oireachtas cultural festival in 1939 and the growth of a new crop of language organisations during the 1940s (many of them concerned with publishing books, magazines and a newspaper) were signs of growing concern among the revivalists, and of a growing realisation that an Irish state, even under the 1937 Constitution, did not necessarily mean the restoration of the language. In 1943 Comhdháil Náisiúnta na Gaeilge was established to co-ordinate the activities of the language organisations. The previous year had seen the first issue of the prestigious magazine *Comhar*, and this was followed within the decade by the founding of *Inniu* and *Feasta*. The 1950s and 1960s saw no slackening in the growth of new language organisations. In 1963 Eoin McKiernan counted 'a minimum of 16 major national organisations founded since 1940 for the promotion of particular aspects of the revival'.[5] These organisations included Na Teaghlaigh Gaelacha and Cumann na Sagart, an organisation which has had an important influence within the Catholic Church, and which has also sponsored the *Glór na nGael* competition to encourage the use of Irish as a community language. Perhaps the most consistently innovative of the new organisations has been Gael-Linn, founded in 1953. Not only has Gael-Linn shown imagination in raising funds, but it has extended the language front into such areas as documentary films, records and cassettes, drama, youth festivals and the manufacture and marketing of native Irish crafts. Many of these activities, most notably film-making in Irish, pointed up the full measure of state neglect, since recommendations for state initiatives in these areas had been gathering dust on departmental shelves long before 1953.

Even in the areas of direct government responsibility the years since the war have been years of retreat and failure. As late as 1959 over one-third of the Civil Service had little or no Irish, while in Gaeltacht areas almost half the public servants were incompetent in Irish.[6] The status of the language in the institutions of state and in such semi-state bodies as Aer Lingus and Bord Fáilte is a useful index of the state's earnestness in the revival effort. The limited use of the Irish language in the conduct of business in the houses of the Oireachtas is, perhaps, the best indication of 'establishment' attitudes. It is hardly surprising, in view of the state's record on the language issue, that Irish has made so little headway in the commercial or industrial life of the country. Indeed, the wonder is that it has made any progress at all. The influence of the state-controlled television has worked steadily against the revival policy. In this context it is interesting to refer to what one observer had to say in 1963 when Irish TV was in its infancy and the impact of economic expansion could not yet be estimated:

> But two new developments pose problems to try the state's sincerity: TV and the economic expansion program. Either, or jointly, *these* are destined to be touchstones of government honesty and initiative with regard to the language. Either, or jointly, these can become the most formidable opponents of the revival.[7]

The last fifteen years have provided an answer to the query implicit in these comments.

The state has not been unaware of the deteriorating condition of the revival policy, nor has it wanted for advice. In 1963 a government commission issued a lengthy report, the first serious, if rather soft, critical appraisal of the revival policy. Its main conclusion was that 'there could be no survival without revival', and the report made many specific recommendations. A government White Paper gave a general blessing to the report.[8] But few of its recommendations were implemented with any degree of conviction. The procession of advisory bodies continued. In 1969 Comhairle na Gaeilge was set up to advise the government on the revival policy. This was followed within a few years by Bord na Gaeilge which is still with us. Notwithstanding the useful work and high dedication of the officers of these bodies they do not as yet seem to have had any demonstrable influence on the condition of crisis in which the language revival policy finds itself.

Indeed, even in the area where the state placed most of its revivalist hopes from the very outset, that is to say, the schools, the evidence suggests that the position of the language has deteriorated since the war, and deteriorated rather sharply in the last decade. Already by the late 1940s many teachers were

expressing doubts and frustrations at what they saw as the unreasonable demands being made on the schools to carry the
language revival policy almost on their own, with no apparent
back-up from any other sector. The requirement that Irish be
essential for state examinations was a live political issue from at
least 1949. The lack of textbooks and other essential aids in
language-teaching gradually began to take its toll on the morale
in the schools. The decline in the number of A-schools (i.e.
schools where all subjects are taught through Irish) has gone on
uninterrupted since the 1950s, and had reached a critical position
by the early 1970s. The decision in the late 1960s to phase out
the Preparatory Colleges—special second-level colleges where
Irish-speakers were groomed from an early age for a career in
teaching—has deprived the teaching profession of a regular
supply of teachers with high fluency in Irish. At third level
there is a clear sign of the times in the decline in recent years in
the number of courses being taught through Irish in University
College Galway, which has had a special responsibility for Irish
in third level education since the 1920s. There is also clear
evidence of a diminished status for the Irish language in the
curriculum and conduct of business in the teacher-training
colleges. Finally, recently revealed evidence by Liam Andrews
and Dr Colmán Ó hUallacháin confirms what many teachers
and language activists have suspected for some time, namely,
that there has been a serious decline in the status and standard
of Irish in the primary and secondary schools in recent
years.[9]

Ireland's entry into the European Economic Community,
which many people believed would increase popular appreciation of the desirability of a national language, does not seem
to have done so, at least going by the evidence of the schools.
What has increased, however, has been the demand for continental languages, notably French and German. Writing in
1966 Dr Seán Ó Tuama gave as his opinion that 'it is almost
impossible to envisage in the foreseeable future any other language taking the place of Irish as the second vernacular taught
in our educational system'.[10] It is debatable if that statement
could be made with any conviction twelve years later.

It is an interesting, if sad, paradox that while this deterioration in the position of Irish in post-war Ireland has been

taking place, the evidence of census, of attitude surveys, and of a more casual kind (e.g. the popularity of certain Irish-language TV shows) point to widespread public good-will towards the language, or at the very least, to an affirmation of public desire that it should not be allowed to die.[11] To translate this benign passivity into something more positive called for expert linguistic planning, and political will and energy. For a brief period during the 1960s the expertise and the instruments for enlightened linguistic planning were available to the state, but recent disclosures by Dr Ó hUallacháin suggest that a paralysis of political will allied to bureaucratic obstruction combined to abort any such planning.[12] Perhaps this should be seen as part of the general lack of confidence in planning of any sort which characterised the early 1970s. Certainly, the decision in 1973 to drop Irish as an essential subject for the Leaving Certificate and the Civil Service removed the last vestige of state policy on the language, and it is scarcely an exaggeration to say that at the present time there is a greater lack of direction in the state's attitude towards the language question than at any time since 1922.

There is further sad irony in the fact that as the language revival and the condition of the Gaeltacht entered a deep crisis during the past thirty years, modern Irish writing, has experienced something of a renaissance, with a number of writers of the very first rank (Ó Cadhain in prose, and the poets Ó Direáin and Ó Ríordáin), and a further group of lesser but nonetheless significant talents. Of course by 1950 the groundwork for a modern literature in Irish had already been laid sufficiently well to justify two anthologies—*Nuafhilíocht* (1950) and *Nuascéalaíocht* (1952)—the literary fruits of the revival. 1950 also saw the publication of Ó Cadhain's *Cré na Cille*, and the next twenty-five years were to see him and others bend, fashion and enrich the language to make it respond to all the demands and nuances of a writer's experience in a modern urbanised society. Many of the younger writers are not only bilingual writers (e.g. Eoghan Ó Tuairisc, and Criostóir Ó Floinn), but they have also shown considerable versatility in various forms of writing—poetry, drama and prose. Again we may note Ó Floinn, Ó Tuairisc, Diarmuid Ó Súilleabháin, Siobhán Ní Shúilleabháin and Seán Ó Tuama, to mention but a few. The language itself has been standardised

in spelling and grammar. Inevitably, however, even the most challenging of the modern Irish writers have felt the pressures and the
doubts caused by the deteriorating language situation. Let Ó
Cadhain speak for them all, as he did in *Páipéir Bhána agus
Páipéir Bhreaca* in 1969:

Tá rud níos measa ná an t-uireasa aitheantais sa mbaile agus
i gcéin ag goilliúint ar an scríbhneoir. Is deacair do dhuine
a dhícheall a dhéanamh i dteanga arb é a cosúlacht go
mbeidh sí básaithe roimhe féin má fhaigheann sé cúpla
bliain eile saoil.[13]

[There is yet a worse fate for the Irish writer than the lack
of recognition at home and abroad. It is difficult for a man
to give of his best in a language which, it seems, may be dead
sooner than himself, if he is spared a few more years.]

Whatever the problems confronting the post-war Irish writer
writing in English, at least he is spared this harrowing spectre
of the imminent death of the language in which he is writing.
We may well ask what exactly were these problems and concerns facing the Irish writer in English?

After the claustrophobia of the 1940s it was probably inevitable that Irish writers and artists in the post-war era would
rush to open the shutters to the outside world, straining after
cosmopolitan themes and concerns. Of course, there had never
been total darkness. Throughout the 1940s *The Bell* had kept
vigil for the freedom of the Irish writer, and when its run ended
in 1954 there were already clear signs that changes were taking
place in state and public attitudes towards such issues as censorship and artistic freedom. These changes in public attitudes and
sensibility have been accelerating during the past fifteen years,
so that to an Irish reader of the mid-1970s the furore which
followed the publication of Eric Cross's *Tailor and Ansty* in the
1940s seems now to belong to old unhappy far-off things and
battles long ago. Certainly, as the revolution in transport and
communications has drawn Ireland into the global village since
the 1960s, there has been an exciting variety and vitality of theme
and treatment, in all forms of Irish writing and art.

Though literary works can never be treated as mere historical
documents, it is nevertheless the case that Irish writing has

mirrored the major changes in Irish society since the 1950s—emigration and rural depopulation, urbanisation, increasing social mobility, the questioning of frail old gods and of strange new ones, of old dogmas and new fashions. The emigrant trail since the war has, of course, been predominantly eastwards, to the industrial centres of Britain. And, while Brian Friel's *Philadelphia, here I come!* poignantly captures the choice and conflict between the ties and pieties of the old world and the lure of the good life on the shores of Amerikay, the more representative emigrants of post-war Ireland are Edna O'Brien's country girls, the lads and lambs of Tom Murphy and Cristóir Ó Floinn, and, of course, Dónal Mac Amhlaigh's heroic breed of navvies.[14]

The 'urban' experience has become the experience of an ever-increasing proportion of Irish citizens during the past twenty years. In literature, the sights, sounds and smells of the city of Anna Livia had already been celebrated by the 1930s, and by the late 1940s O'Connor and Ó Faoláin had paid their homage to Cork. In post-war writing the 'city' has been the teeming, strumpet city of James Plunkett and Christy Browne; Brendan Kennelly's Dublin of 'treacherous talk' and 'malignant silences', Basil Payne's Dublin, the poise and elegance of the urbane world of Terence de Vere White. It is also Brian Moore's strife-torn Belfast, the ranting city of Sam Thompson's evangelists, Michael Longley's 'city of guns and long knives'. The city experience is also Séamas Deane's long-suffering Derry:

> The unemployment in our bones
> Erupting on our hands in stones;
> The thoughts of violence a relief;
> The act of violence a grief;
> Our bitterness and love
> Hand in glove.[15]

And, of course, there are the other less anguished witnesses: the cosy post-war Galway of Ó hEithir's *Lig Sinn i gCathú* and the hidden passions of John Broderick's Athlone.

But the city is also, in Ireland as elsewhere, the haven and the prison of the uprooted and alienated refugees, so well described in Máirtín Ó Díreáin's *Ár Ré Dhearóil*:

Tá cime romham
Tá cime i mo dhiaidh
Is mé féin ina lár
I mo chime mar chách,
Is a Dhia Mhóir
Fóir ar na céadta againn
Ó d'fhágamar slán
Ag talamh ag trá
Tóg de láimh sinn
Idir fheara is mhná
Sa chathair fhallsa.[16]

[Captives before and behind me/And I myself in the middle, a captive like the rest/O Great God, protect the hundreds of us, since we said farewell to land and beach/Take us in hand, men and women, in this deceiving city.]

In a rapidly changing society, with rising mobility and significant shifts in popular attitudes and sensibilities, it was inevitable that the rites of passage from adolescence to adulthood—the three crises of 'faith, sex and culture' as one critic has called it[17]—should feature prominently in post-war Irish writing. Again, Brian Moore's Judith Hearne and Gavin Burke come to mind, as do McGahern's autobiographical insights, and, of course, Edna O'Brien's country girls. Indeed, in their own way the writings of Ms O'Brien offer biographical notes for the age.[18]

Not all has changed, of course. The land, with its elemental passions, its timeless social relationships, the land remains. The land as Heaney's geological deposit of identity, the land as the metaphor of Eugene McCabe's study in human cruelty, and, magnificently, the land as the great obsession of John B. Keane's Bull McCabe.[19] The drama of village tensions in Tom Kilroy's *Big Chapel* gives notice of the enduring interest in rural hierarchies. And this scarcely begins to suggest the variety of post-war Irish writing. It is indeed a remarkable span of perception and reference which runs from Ben Kiely's 'mountain streams' to Neil Jordan's *Night in Tunisia*.

Inevitably, the recurring problem of the 'Irish identity' has been brought into sharp and tragic focus by the war in the North during the past decade. The identity problem has been particularly acute for a gifted group of northern writers, mainly poets, who have produced an extraordinary rich harvest since the 1950s, and especially during the past fifteen years.[20]

The post-war Irish theatre has had a chequered history. On the credit side we may cite the vigorous amateur drama movement, the continued stimulus (despite many ups and downs) of the Dublin Theatre Festival since its beginning in 1958, the opening of the new Abbey Theatre in 1966, the survival and standards of the Gate Theatre and the resilience and courage of non-establishment theatre in Dublin and the provinces. If by special dispensation we include the impact of native sons on world theatre then we may justly claim a front seat for Samuel Beckett. On the home front, however, it is not unfair to say that post-war Irish theatre has not set the sky ablaze, though we have had a respectable cluster of stars, and in Brendan Behan we did supply a short-lived tragic meteor.[21]

What I have said of the men of letters applies also, in a general way, to other Irish artists in the post-war era. The elements of continuity and change, of the traditional and the innovative, are well-represented. In art it is possible to discern two main currents since the 1940s, running if not in tandem at least in fruitful complementarity—the traditional school of the RHA (with its strength in landscapes, portraits, fine craftsmanship and representational sculpture) and, since the foundation of the Living Art Exhibition in 1943, a less conventional, more experimental, more abstract movement. As Bruce Arnold has written: 'The range and diversity of the work of artists active in Ireland in the period since 1960 is immense.'[22]

Likewise in music and ballet the spectrum runs from folk-ballet to Boydell and Bodley, with the gifted Prospero Ó Riada fusing all strands in the fertile cave of his imagination.

In sum, post-war Irish artists have discovered that in opening the shutters the window allows not only a view to the outside world but also a new light through to the interior. What one critic has said of John Montague's poetic concerns probably covers the main thrust of Irish literature in both languages, and of Irish artistic life in general, as we move into the last quarter of the twentieth century. Terence Brown speaks of Montague's two persistent concerns as being 'to comprehend his native place, and to respond to the contemporary world without parochial evasion'.[23] It is a challenging prospect.

E

NOTES

1. In 1968 the government of the day granted tax exemption to certain categories of creative artists living and working in Ireland.
2. For background see e.g. B. Ó Cuív, *Irish Dialects and Irish-speaking Districts*, Dublin 1971; S. Ó Tuama (ed.), *The Gaelic League Idea*, (1972); B. Ó Cuív (ed.), *A View of the Irish Language*, (1969). The most recent reliable data is that collected during field-work by Deasún Fennell in 1975. Mr Fennell has kindly allowed me access to this information.
3. This demand was not new. See, for example. *A Board for the Gaeltacht* Comhdháil Náisiúnta na Gaeilge, 1953; Also, *Polasaí na Gaeltachta* Conradh na Gaeilge, 1976.
4. Eoin McKiernan, *The Will of a Nation*, St Paul, 1963, 2.
5. *Ibid.*, 3.
6. Cited by F. S. L. Lyons, *Ireland since the Famine*, (1973), 637.
7. McKiernan, *op. cit.*, 10.
8. Commission on the Restoration of the Irish Language : Summary of the Final Report, Dublin 1963. Also, The Restoration of the Irish Language : Government White Paper, Dublin 1965.
9. L. S. Andrews, A *Black Paper on Irish Education: The decline of Irish as a school subject in the Republic of Ireland 1967–77*, An Conradh Ceilteach 1978. Colmán Ó hUallacháin speaking to Timlín Ó Cearnaigh on *Radio na Gaeltachta*, 28 Feb. 1978 and 3 Mar. 1978.
10. S. Ó Tuama (ed.), *The Gaelic League Idea*, 105.
11. See for example, *An Coiste um Thaighde ar dhearcadh an Phobail i dtaobh na Gaeilge: Tuarascáil*, Oifig an Rialtais 1976.
12. See Ó hUallacháin tapes cited in note 9.
13. Máirtín Ó Cadhain, *Páipéir Bhána agus Páipéir Bhreaca*, 1969, 40.
14. See, for example, Edna O'Brien, *The Country Girls* (1960), *The Lonely Girl* (1962); Tom Murphy, *Whistle in the Dark* (1961); Criostóir Ó Floinn, *The Lambs* (RTE play 1967); Dónal Mac Amhlaigh, *Dialann Deoraí* (1960).
15. S. Deane, *Derry*, cited in Pádraic Fiacc (ed.), *The Wearing of the Black*, Belfast 1974, 53.
16. Máirtín Ó Direáin, *Ár Ré Dhearóil* (1962), II.
17. John Wilson Foster, *Forces and Themes in Ulster Fiction* (1974), 118.
18. Brian Moore, *The Lonely Passion of Judith Hearne* (1955),

The Emperor of Ice-cream (1965); John McGahern, *The Barracks* (1963), *The Dark* (1965).

19. Eugene McCabe, *King of the Castle* (1964); J. B. Keane, *The Field* (1965); For Heaney see Terence Brown, *Northern Voices* (1975), 171–186. See also, Robert Buttuel, *Seamas Heaney* (1975).

20. See Brown, *Northern Voices*; J. Wilson Foster, *op. cit.* For an anthology see Padraic Fiacc (ed.), *The Wearing of the Black* (1974).

21. For Behan see C. Kearney, *The Writings of Brendan Behan* (1977).

22. Bruce Arnold, *A Concise history of Irish Art*, (1977), 167.

23. Brown, *op. cit.*, 149.

The Media, 1945-70

Douglas Gageby

The Irish communications world at the end of World War II was, by today's standards, extremely circumscribed. Your morning newspaper, for example, could have been four pages. When I first became a journalist on *The Irish Press* in June 1945, that was the daily ration, and I still remember the fuss that arose when suddenly we had to produce a six-page paper. We hardly knew what to do with the space.

Life, in general, had been circumscribed during our neutrality. It was not newsprint alone that was short, nor tea and sugar; there was oil and petrol, and coal for the railways. A journey from Dublin to the south could take fifteen hours by train, with frequent stops for cleaning out the cinders. So, even the distribution of news was difficult.

Irish radio had not become a regular and major source of news. The first bulletin of the day came at noon. It was to be many years before we reached the on-the-hour and half-hour radio news to which we are now accustomed. There was no television, of course.

There was BBC radio, and all Europe, too, was listening. German radio meant Lord Haw Haw and William Joyce.

Nor were there so many listeners or radio sets. The highest licence figure during the war was 183,000 in 1941. That figure fell later, not because of lack of interest, but because rural radio depended on batteries which were hard to get. In 1944, it was estimated that only 13 per cent of households in rural areas had wireless sets and 52 per cent in the larger towns. It was 1947 before the licence figures rose again to the 1941 figure. in 1978 the figure for television licences was approximately 600,000.

It is remarkable to us today that native Irish governments,

urging a return to the well-springs of knowledge and custom of our ancestors, should have left the airwaves unworked, and thus open to the BBC, for want of sufficient programmes of our own. The BBC programmes may have been good but the message they carried was seldom the message an Irish government would have wished. Given equally available Irish and British programmes, the listener could have made his choice; for long, there was one channel only, to use the TV term, for many many hours of the day. Our service gave about five and a half hours broadcasting in twenty-four.

The news itself had not been an undiluted quantity, certainly as far as newspapers were concerned. Censorship in Ireland was more heavy-handed than that of any other neutral. This probably had an effect on both the press and the public for some years after.

Our censors not only hacked solidly at the real war of news, to make sure that we gave a cautiously neutral account of the fighting no matter who was winning but they took care that no information on what was going on in the twenty-six counties, which might remotely be useful to either belligerent, should disgrace our newspapers.

So, the great freeze up of 1943/4 which turned Phoenix Park ponds into skating rinks, which brought a whole Swiss wintersports atmosphere to the country, could not be recorded in picture or word. A foot of snow on 9 May is something that might go into the annals; it didn't get into the newspapers or onto the air in that same year of 1943 because it was 'military' information.

Of course, servants of the nearest belligerent had only to take a boat to Dun Laoghaire, or send a plane across, or get a tip from the daily cross-channel travellers (phones were tapped, naturally) but we were playing a game according to the rules very strictly indeed.

It all may look bizarre now, but it was surprising what the British and American press could make out of a weekend visit to Dublin.

Neutrality left serious effects on the whole country and the news media were touched particularly. We were less informed than almost any other people in Western Europe. Unlike other neutrals, we had no correspondents from Irish newspapers or

from Irish radio reporting from outside. After the war, correspondents did go out to report on the wreckage. Irish war correspondents could have been an embarrassment, politically, of
course, to such a strict observance of the rules as journalists often
are.

All news services were filtered through London; this was an
old complaint going back to Arthur Griffith's day, and, some
would say to Giraldus Cambrensis. We did little about it in the
past, but today television helps us leap that paper wall which
for long loomed so large in our politics. Later we will be looking
at one official attempt to breach it.

The journalists of thirty years ago were a different breed.
Today everyone knows journalists. They can be seen on television, their by-lines recognised in newspapers and they may be
met on social and newsworthy occasions. They are no different
from anyone else.

Thirty years ago journalists seldom wrote under their own
names. They were anonymous, less numerous and less visible
on the horizon. There were few graduates around yet there was
a barrister or two, often as editor or in one of the other senior
jobs. These were by no means men fated to be briefless barristers,
rather men who had looked at life in the courts and had thrown
their lot in with a craft, an art, a trade that has its own even
more arcane delights than the majesty of the law.

And there was perhaps a *gravitas* which is not so common
today. They could be rancorous in defence of the right to do the
job. One of them even went to jail for his pains.

This is not to say that journalistic standards of today have
slipped. Journalists now are better educated. Perhaps panache
has to some extent been dimmed. It was an ill-paid calling
thirty years ago but not so today. Today we live less on the
sidelines of society than journalists did thirty years ago, and
so we may miss some of the perspectives granted to the more
detached observers of the past.

What did the world of communications consist of in the late
1940s? It was 1952 before the Irish radio emitted an 8 a.m.
news bulletin, and that was during a newspaper strike. It was
1966 when the system went over to all day broadcasting.

As to the quality of news which came from it, at the begin-
ing of our period, Maurice Gorham, who was Director of Broad-

casting from 1953 to 1960, has recorded that the station in fact had no paid news service at all in 1945, but picked up its information 'from a variety of sources without acknowledgement or payment', and had done so for twenty years. This meant, for one thing, good shorthand for the taking down of BBC bulletins; and as there is no copyright in fact, Irish radio got away with two decades of piracy. But in 1946 the money was provided for staff and for the purchase of a proper service of foreign news through the Press Association in London.

There then began the recruiting of more staff, inside and outside the station. It was to be years before Irish radio became something more than a fractious section of the Department of Posts and Telegraphs, and, after loosening the reins in the 1950s, achieved its present semi-autonomous status under a broadcasting authority, a broadcasting act and a minister.

That was radio. There was no television as we have already noted, and the backbone of the newspaper press was, according to your bent, the national press, publishing mostly in Dublin, or the provincial press, which covered the local scene, usually once weekly, and which is fortunately still a vital and creative part not only of the media world but of the whole of Irish society.

What is loosely called the national press is really the Dublin press—largely circulating in the twenty-six counties, largely concerned with twenty-six county events, but sending enough copies into the North to justify, in some eyes, the term 'national'.

Furthermore these papers have also to be local papers, for Ireland is a small country. We want to know what townsland a man comes from and who his wife's people are—facts, human details. And, of course, we have to know how the French economy is going and what the CIA is up to in South America. We make demands on our papers.

The Independent Group was the largest corpus to be seen; morning paper, *The Irish Independent*; evening paper, *The Evening Herald*, which largely confined itself to Dublin and Leinster; and *The Sunday Independent*. *The Irish Times* in Westmoreland Street, publishing also *The Times Pictorial*, a weekly and *The Field*, a racing journal, likewise weekly.

The Irish Press was not yet a group. It published only the daily *Irish Press*, yet with a spurt coming on, which was to bring it level with, and later ahead of, the Independent group in sales. One would look far for a comparable achievement in publishing. Eighteen years after launching, shakily enough it seemed at the time, a new daily *The Irish Press* was to publish in 1949 a Sunday newspaper whose sales for years have topped that of any Irish journal. Then, five years later, *The Evening Press* was to come, and there was an interesting sociological background to this enterprise.

For now and again in newspaper circles someone would aver that the natural daily newspaper for a country which was largely agricultural, was an evening paper. Arthur Griffith was one man on whom the saying was fathered. A.E. was another. No matter, the difficulty had always been that of distribution. How do you land an up-to-date newspaper, printed in Dublin, at the nearest shop to a Kerry schoolteacher as he wends his way home in the afternoon, or a factory worker in Antrim? An answer had been provided by a Mr Bush whose compact machine enabled late news to be printed locally. It was superimposed into a newspaper which had been published hours before in Dublin, yet left something like two columns open on the front page for this later edition.

So far, Dublin evening newspapers, the *Herald* and the *Evening Mail*, (the latter since dead), had perforce been confined to the Pale, and to small numbers despatched by direct rail to some provincial centres. *The Evening Press* saw the whole of the island as a circulation area. Its success was not immediate but it was convincing and at its highest circulation figure, it still is a bit short of the biggest morning paper sale, *The Irish Independent*. *The Evening Herald* responded to the challenge.

But nothing stands still in the communications world. As radio enlarged its coverage, as racing news and stock exchange news and other items came hourly off the air, the Dublin evenings were outpaced. It is outside our period, but a couple of years ago, and twenty years after the experiment started, the last Bush printing station closed. And yet—strange reciprocity and durability of the trade—these two papers still span the country as do the morning ones, with apparently no loss of circulation.

As to other newspapers, there are thirty-nine members of the Provincial Newspapers Association of Ireland, covering the twenty-six counties; they include almost all of the provincial papers published. As with the national press, they share a distinction which singles out this country from all its EEC partners. This is the only member state in which there is no subsidisation for newspapers as a public service. In other countries publishers may get concessions in cheaper postage, cheaper telegraph rates, and even direct subsidies. Alone, in Ireland, the newspapers are not only unbuttressed, but they pay a heavy rate of VAT on cover and on advertising. British papers come in here, in great numbers; in their country of origin they are zero-rated for VAT.

Some of the provincial papers are hard pressed. An enlightened government might see in them one of the essential props of a rural infrastructure, which national policy is apparently committed to retain where possible. We know how the loss of a school, a church, a Garda station in a rural area may be only the first trickle in an avalanche. A local paper, attentive to the life around it, is one of the great safeguards, and one notable means of promoting local self-respect.

The journalist trained in the provincial office starts with an immeasurable advantage. He or she—and it is very often she nowadays—has learned the trade from the bottom. He or she has reported courts, visited bereaved families, covered sports matches, written paragraphs for the gossip column, walked muddy ground as farmers explained their tribulations. He or she has seen the physical putting together of the paper and may even have delivered copies to the local newsagent. Intensive, practical training—and on publication day, he or she walks down the main street to face the people who have been attacked or flattered in print. It is good training, not because one learns caution, but because one learns scrupulosity and accuracy.

Ireland may sometimes be accused of being isolationist, reclusive, indifferent to the world outside. Our normal reaction to such a charge is to recall the missionaries of the early centuries of Irish christianity, the Wild Geese, the diaspora of the famine years, to point to our million Irish-born now living in Britain. We are sensitive though, to what the outside world says of us, and the Paper Wall referred to before is a phrase that has been in our period almost as commonly used as 'The Evils of Partition' or 'The Twin National Aspirations'.

The Paper Wall was, it was argued, erected by Britain,

through whom alone the world could get a picture of Ireland. For England owned the newspapers that captured the attention of the world, England had the news agencies which circulated by wire and radio the current intelligence about this part of the world that the rest of the world read.

It was a fair enough assessment. In 1950 there began an experiment which aimed at punching a hole in the newspaper wall—surely an achievement worth aiming at. The experiment was called The Irish News Agency.

Now, as most people know today, every country has at least one organisation which gathers, collates, and sells further on the news from all its towns, cities and component parts. The biggest, like the Associated Press of America, are commercial concerns, based on the news-gathering potential of their client members (i.e. newspapers and electric media) and often backed by government aid, usually in the shape of cheaper facilities. Other well known agencies are Agence France Presse, United Press International and Reuters.

Now, although governments are drawn in on various stages of the operations of such news agencies, it must not be seen to be too obviously a government initiative or largely government-run. That would be a propaganda agency. To be good, a news agency needs to be run by professionals, and, in free enterprise societies, with proprietorial newspaper interests giving a great part of the backing.

But the Irish News Agency never stimulated proprietors here to take a major part. It caused suspicion among journalists whose sideline earnings on correspondence for English or American papers seemed to be threatened and it was entirely government-funded, so that it was easily labelled a mere propaganda machine.

It died in 1958. Ten or twelve years later it would have been of value not only to Ireland, but to the world press when the North became major news because acceptance as a regular news agency means acceptance of the words you send on the wire day by day, about the trivial as well as the important, the scandalous as well as the elevating.

On major news stories, newspapers, radio and television stations send their own men to cover. But the greater part of the daily news they receive comes from sources such as the Irish

News Agency hoped to be—regular, reliable, naturally coloured by the country of its origin, but as to fact, beyond cavil. Prestige articles in reputable journals help a country's image, but the daily flow of facts, good, bad and indifferent, are what the world goes by.

Sean MacBride, then Minister for External Affairs, and former newspaperman, launched the idea. It died, not without honour but with so much unfulfilled. One can be cynical and say that a news agency is, like a national airline, a badge prerequisite for modern nationality but it is also a service not only to one's own country, but to one's neighbours.

The gap in not having a national news agency is as inexplicable as the empty airwaves of the 1920s, 1930s and 1940s. And the trade or industry itself has nothing to be proud of. No merchant adventurers, and indeed no visionaries, were around the newspaper world of the 1950s.

We have considered something of the form of the Irish media in our period and should look more to the content. For a long time Irish newspapers were more conservative than, say, the French or British press; that is, more reticent, less sensational and less inclined to bash at established reputations. This was a matter not only of taste, but of concern for a litigious populace— and litigation is one of the great unsung sports of Irish life.

The newspapers were easily defined in their political outlook. *The Irish Press* was clearly on the side of its founder, Eamon de Valera; the Independent Group aligned roughly with the former Cumann na nGael party, but did not openly commit itself; *The Irish Times* enjoyed taking its pick. But, overall, the kind of coverage was the same : recording more than analysing, criticising but not often taking apart, and generally over-concentrating on the twenty-six counties area to the exclusion not only of world affairs, but of the affairs of the rest of the country.

To tell you what has happened in the last twenty-four hours is a fair task for any newspaper. What is called campaigning journalism sometimes consists in telling you what one writer thinks, to the exclusion of what actually happens; but analysis is a necessary concomitant to recording. If the late 1940s was a period of recovery from a laming neutrality, the 1950s were dull and inconsequent.

In 1959 there came an economic wind to emulate the spiritual wind of John XXIII. The famous Green Paper drawn up by Kenneth Whitaker and enthusiastically sponsored by the Taoiseach, Sean Lemass, seemed, consequently or not, to usher in a new era. The wind of religion was soon to sweep through the columns of Irish newspapers, with a young man, John Horgan, now a member of the Dáil, writing about Vatican II and the ecclesiastical changes with close knowledge, compassion and with sympathy.

Religion was all at once an absorbing topic and not really frightening if you grasped the nettle tightly. The correspondence columns of the newspapers, and especially of *The Irish Times*, had controversy as vivid as a letter from St Paul.

Gone was the day when religious reporting consisted of reproducing sermons, speeches or pastorals verbatim. 'In full or not at all' was the usual condition of one ecclesiastic when he sent his pastorals to the newspapers. The religious correspondent of the 1960s was as adventurous, as incisive, and as questioning as his political colleagues had become.

The introduction of an irreverent assessment of politicians was largely initiated in a tabloid newspaper, *The Sunday Review*, which died a decade before another Sunday tabloid came to make the grade successfully. *The Sunday Review* was a tabloid, but of an unusual kind perhaps; it was one of the few newspapers in Europe to publish in full the encyclical *Mater et Magistra*. An irreverent approach to politicians is not incompatible with a serious regard for the institutions. Yet a good deal of reality has been lost through the proliferation of scripts or speeches issued in advance. It makes for lazy journalism and it allows politicians, when reporters fail to turn up at the meeting to check delivery of the speech, to be two-faced. The script as published may be bland, the actual words delivered bearing little relation to the sanitised prose.

The scene was set for television. It arrived on the last day of 1961. It could bring a live bishop or a spluttering politician in front of our eyes; and because television from across the water and across the border was, anyway, importing ideas and pictures that were shocking yet stimulating, our television had to do the same. Not that there was anything half-hearted about Irish television when it arrived. It sometimes only needed to put an assortment of Irish people in a studio and wait for the sound of crashing idols.

Gay Byrne, himself no radical, did prodigious work in opening up areas of debate for the populace as a whole which had hitherto been confined to the more rarified columns of the print world. His method was to bring protagonists into the studio, and ask blunt questions with disarming politeness. What at first seemed blasphemous or obscene, very soon was taken to the heart of the viewing public as ordinary tea-time chat.

A good press reflects and records; that is its function. And it is quite an achievement to get most things right most of the time; but a good press also stimulates, prods, reminds and leads. It has a restless conscience; it is constructive and imaginative.

How well by these yardsticks did the media do in the quarter-century we are describing? We are an agricultural country, yet talk of production and expansion was so often pinned on factories, imported and sometimes fly-by-night. The great mineral wealth—which we were told at school did not exist—began to be exploited; but only at the end of the quarter-century, when EEC was on the horizon, did many of us begin to appreciate the wealth in the soil itself. There were always a few stout hearts to remind us that in the seas around us was untold wealth—but we had to go and fish for it. One cannot recall any great press campaigns.

Sociological reporting is today's term for looking at human beings in their various plights. We might all earlier have questioned the effect on Irish society of the stripping away of the people from the land. John Healy wrote a series of articles that later became a book entitled *The Death of an Irish Town*. This came in the last years only of our period. A whole new world of cool clinical reporting came from Michael Viney, with novel studies of unmarried mothers, alcoholics, deprived children and other castaways of the 1960s.

Then there was what we now call The North. It used to appear as 'partition' and was a useful standby for the peroration of a speech, but as to the people who lived behind that partition, their daily roundabout, their jobs, the way they spent their leisure, their arts and sports, there was very little. Once in a while there would be a big story about unemployment in the Belfast shipyards, regularly a bitter piece of invective from one side or the other. One seldom met anyone who had been there. It really *was* behind a partition.

Late in our period, however, it began to intrude. After a series of border shootings had died down in the early 1960s, Sean Lemass one day ran up in his car and had a talk and a meal with Terence O'Neill, the Northern Prime Minister. There was surprise in the South, some head-shaking but mostly reaction was on the right side.

In the North, among the Unionists, there was delayed action and then murder—literally. Unionism was never to be the same again. The place began to be noticed. Dublin papers had been gingerly exploring it, sending what were almost foreign correspondents into the blackest parts. There was a parliament wasn't there? An infamous body. Some papers began to report it as they reported the other parliament in Dublin. Things were moving forward. But they were moving backward too. As rioting became guerilla warfare, the television cameras of the world came to see—and they are still around.

And how was the real communications world up there? It included both BBC television and radio and Independent television. In Belfast the big evening paper, *The Telegraph*, was bought over by Lord Thomson, a deal that was much resented in the city and which left a bad taste in Thomson's mouth too, for he had been accused of sharp practice. *The Northern Whig*, once a liberal paper, died; its morning rival, the Unionist *News Letter*, and believed to be the oldest daily sheet in these islands. persisted (its only rival now is *The Irish News*, the organ of the Nationalist population).

Like the Republic, the North has a healthy local press, touched up here and there with modern colour, but earthy and racy too.

The national and provincial press and the official broadcasting system, cover the greater part of the media system. Weekly journals of opinion, monthly and quarterly publications have also played their part. *The Bell* (which started before 1945) was edited by Sean O'Faolain and later by Peadar O'Donnell. Apart from its own rugged contributions to controversy, it pioneered a documentary style of reporting which the newspapers were slow enough to follow. *Studies*, the Jesuit quarterly, was consistently sound and occasionally explosive, as with a famous reassessment of Patrick Pearse. *The Leader*, D. P. Moran's old paper, wended its own quiet way, occasionally sending out sparks. *Hibernia*, a monthly, later a fortnightly, and only recently a weekly looks fair set to hold its place. *The Furrow*, from Maynooth, turned up more than a few treasures.

The media and communications world was vigorous enough a quarter of a century after World War II. Radio and television were in a special reserved position. The rest were exposed to the winds of competition, with, for example, one English newspaper being sold in the thirty-two counties for every two Irish morning newspapers.

Today in the EEC, Irish newspapers are the least privileged in the whole nine-country community. Postal concessions, the norm in Europe, telephone and telegraph concessions and other supports are unknown here.

The press survives however. Dublin has three morning news-papers, three Sunday papers and two evening ones. Cork has a morning and evening paper of its own and Belfast has two morn-ing, one evening and one Sunday newspaper.

Variety of choice is good for the reader, and, with all due respects to the electronic media, the need to 'read all about it' is still among us.

Irish Foreign Policy, 1949-69

T. D. Williams

The foreign policy of states is of course determined by a number of factors: by economic interest, geographical location and military power: also by their past history and by present events. Foreign policy is also shaped by intangible and imponderable issues such as the general concept of what foreign policy should be and also in many cases what is called diplomatic tradition. All these elements play a part in forming attitudes of neighbouring states, in particular to Ireland, and in influencing Irish attitudes towards them.

The present president of the state, Dr Hillery, once delivered himself in his capacity of foreign minister, of a long analysis of the principles on which he thought Irish foreign relations should be based. That speech of 18 April 1972 was a penetrating exposition of Irish policy during most of the twenty-year period here under survey. Hillery referred, in particular, to three issues which, according to him, dominated any country's relations with the world. These are: the assertion of the identity of the state; the recognition of that identity by others, and the promotion and development of exchanges—by trade and by information—with other nations. Because each has been emphasised by a particular phase in our history as an independent state, they have been in a sense the principle issues in our foreign policy but they are not in themselves describable as foreign policy—they signify rather the general aim of Irish foreign relations.

The foreign policy of any Irish government at any particular time is not, so Hillery argued, a single attitude but a network of every kind. We do not make sweeping decisions on foreign policy in the abstract and then see how we can realise them. Decisions should be generally individual and concrete, related to specific issues. Each case should be taken on its own merits. For a small country like Ireland the role of government is not to try and improve a 'grand policy design'. Small states cannot afford that kind of luxury. Their safe role is rather to direct and develop extending contacts in accordance with general ideas of what we stand for or which we wish to achieve. Policy is therefore largely pragmatic, but it is not supposed to be Machiavellian.

The same minister emphasised that what is obvious to the practitioner is not always to students of international theory—namely that states are never wholly free in relation to the policy which they follow. Policy is limited because no state can act against the general philosophy and moral belief of its people and on the other hand because that state must observe the limits circumscribing it—geographic, economic and ideological situations in the world. What states are really free to do is always subject to some restrictions and constraint. Therefore two principle points arise for a small state : policy cannot be a single, grand design and freedom of action is limited. This does not preclude, and certainly did not preclude in the case of Irish foreign policy during the twenty years 1949–1969 of considerable freedom of choice and variety of decision.

Such were the reasons of state which underlay our foreign policy—or at least might have been expected to influence it in this period from 1949.

Historians often like to concoct periodisations. This can be a useful device though it is sometimes artificial and contrived. Certainly if the years 1949–1970 are taken, then particular milestones emerge. A new period can be said to have started in 1949 with the Declaration of the Republic, the departure of Ireland from the British Commonwealth of Nations and the refusal of the Costello-McBride government to join the North Atlantic Treaty Pact. That period concluded twenty years later in 1969–1970 with the introduction of the Northern Ireland crisis on the world stage of the UN—an event in which a leading part was acted by Dr Hillery. This indeed was the only time during the period that the problem of Northern Ireland looked as if it might become an issue of international moment.

The year 1951 saw the return of de Valera as Taoiseach but not his return as foreign minister. For sixteen years he had

controlled foreign policy; he was now to leave it to Frank Aiken.
It is unlikely that he now interested himself so much in the
shaping of foreign policy as he had previously done. The new
era might well be said to have begun in 1959 with the long
delayed arrival of Sean Lemass as successor to de Valera as
Taoiseach. Then followed a new period which, on the whole,
as far as foreign policy was concerned, stretched for a decade
between 1959 and 1969. 1959 marked the apparent end of
the de Valera era; it was followed by the age of Lemass. Changes
in personalities at the top were to bring about alterations in
policies; and this in particular signified a decline in diplomatic
activity at the UN and an intensification of interest in Europe.
But this was clearly to emerge only later towards the middle of
the 1960s.

The de Valera tradition in foreign policy could be said to
have ranged from 1932 to 1959, if not longer. There were, it
is true, intermittent interruptions during the regime of the first
and second coalitions between 1948 and 1951, and 1954–1957.
But these interruptions were of very little importance as far as
concerned general policy. That seemed still to be dominated
by the Anglo-Irish quarrel and by the renewed war of words
over Partition in Dublin, London and Strasbourg. Indeed there
was even a proposal to hold a World Congress of the Mansion
House All-Party Anti-Partition Committee in Newcastle-upon-
Tyne. One big event, however, had taken place which was to
transform the entire texture of Irish diplomacy in the next few
years. This was the lifting of the Soviet veto on the admission
of Ireland to membership of the United Nations which took
place on 14 December 1955. It might be noted, incidentally,
that despite the continued use of that Soviet veto in previous
years the Polish delegation at the United Nations continually
supported the Irish application. This entry to the UN may or
not have been as significant as the entry to Europe in 1972.
Time perhaps will tell; but that entry lies outside the period of
this essay.

All policy is foreign policy was the view of a celebrated
historian. But in the Irish case (when it comes to putting
questions of a general character) it might just as easily be said
that all policy is internal policy or certainly springs from economic
and financial roots; certainly the Ulster problem and Anglo-

Irish relations are usually more often treated as part of internal history. Anyhow, the aim here is to set aside the Ulster question except in so far as it is specifically influenced by or touches upon international affairs. Two examples may be named:

1. The negative decision of 5 April 1949, regarding NATO; and
2. the debate on Partition which took place at United Nations in 1969 and in which Dr Hillery and the Ambassador, Cornelius Cremin, took part.

These were certainly not world-shaking events but they did reach an international audience.

International relations, indeed, were not at all that dramatic in those twenty years from 1949 to 1969. Happily there were no great wars and there were few dangerous international crises. These were resolved outside United Nations in a number of cases. They did not affect Ireland. There were, however, certain highlights especially in the late 1950s and early 1960s. Ireland became in one year a member of the Security Council. Her Ambassador to the United Nations, Frederick Boland, was appointed president of the General Assembly. During that session Boland, as president, clashed with Nikita Kruschev dramatically, and effectively ruled him out of order. The Irish also played an important role in the various controversies and crises that arose in the Katanga-Congo and Cyprus incidents. Conor Cruise O'Brien too figured prominently here. He had always played an important role behind the scenes in the shaping of Ireland's United Nations policy. His part in the Congo was not, strictly speaking, an immediate Irish affair. But nine Irish soldiers died near Elisabethville; Ireland was one of the powers that took a lead in peace-keeping discussion. Her influence was thought to be out of all proportion to her power. A leading English journalist, analysing the evolution and growth of the General Assembly referred to the domination of the Afro-Irish bloc. There was much exaggeration in this remark, but the partnership of Aiken and Cruise O'Brien worked to the satisfaction of the minister. It was a period also in which the Irish delegation, influenced by Cruise O'Brien, did a magnificent job of public relations.

There are certain obvious questions which will occur to any student of Irish international affairs. Among these questions (they are not exhaustive) the following will certainly be included. To what extent was our foreign policy influenced more by some powers than by others? What was the general trend of Irish attitudes on the big controversial questions of those years?

Was foreign policy more influenced by the USA and Britain, or by Canada, Norway and India, the latter three countries constituting a middle bloc? What was the significance of Boland's connections with Canadians like Pearson and Robertson? What too was his role in the choice as Secretary General of U Thant? Ireland was not a 'third world' power, nor did she belong to the non-aligned faction, though she often voted in United Nations for motions proposed by it. This was manifested by the Irish vote on a whole range of issues including Algeria, neutralisation of Central Europe, disengagement, South West Africa, Hungary, the Middle East, the Indian sub-continent, Nigeria, Biafra, the Portuguese Colonies (Angola and Guinea), Ruanda, Israel, Egypt, Togoland, the Cameroons, Somaliland, West New Guinea, Oman, Aden, the Czechoslovakian crisis. As Cruise O'Brien quoted in his brilliant apologia *To Katanga and Back*: 'An independent "Swedish" line is what we had hoped for.' He also wrote:

Nor did Ireland belong to the so-called 'non aligned' group. She was *sui generis*. For some of us, particularly the younger members of the Department, the ideal of what [continues] constituted good international behaviour was exemplified at this time by Sweden. Sweden's action in the international field was, as we saw it, independent, disinterested, and honourable. The Swedes in international affairs did not spend much time in proclaiming lofty moral principles but they usually acted as men would do who were, in fact, animated by such principles. Their voting record was more eloquent than their speeches. It seemed to contain few or no votes against conscience: few or none of those votes which were cast for reasons of convenience or expediency—not to offend a neighbour or an ally who happens to be in the wrong—and are then justified at the podium by an anguished access of legal scruple. Sweden paid its share, and more than its share, for all the humanitarian and peace-making aspects of the UN work and sent out its men, soldiers or civil servants, on various more or less unpleasant tasks as the work of organisation required.

How far did this view of Sweden represent other members of the delegation : Boland, for example, or Cremin directing the Department from headquarters in Dublin?

Other questions which might be asked concerning the possible influence of the Catholic Church on the shaping of the policy of the state or of individuals in it about, for example, China, Nigeria and Israel. Or to what extent did Aiken hurry on the gradual change in emphasis and nuance expressed in the attitudes of the new Taoiseach, Sean Lemass? Lemass visited New York and the United Nations in 1963; but his heart and his head were far more attached to the new conferences in Brussels than in New York.

A historian would tend, I think, to see Irish foreign policy as developing over this entire period from :

(a) the isolation of war-time neutrality and the immediate post-war period through
(b) the new involvement on the larger international scene in the Council of Europe and the United Nations of the 1950s, to
(c) the beginning of the negotiations for a voluntary commitment to European integration in the 1960s.

In this context the main themes of Irish foreign policy over the whole twenty years could be seen as follows—in succession.

1. The Anti-Partition campaign in the late 1940s and the late 1950s. This proved to be predicated on the erroneous assumption that if we make the wrongs we think we have suffered known, the world will step in to redress them. In fact, the world has taken little enough interest in the propagandist case continually made. It has shown some interest in the violence and the horror that continues.

2. Involvement in the Council of Europe (early 1950s). This, of course, stopped short of any kind of involvement in the embryo EEC. But it did represent a new emergence of an independent Ireland on the international scene after the isolation of the World War II. We tried here to play the anti-Partition card. It did not work.

3. UN membership as from 14 December 1955. Ireland played a notable and, as I think it would be generally agreed, a responsible but naturally minor role in the years 1956 to 1960. It was possible to do so then because the polarisation of the Cold War left a useful mediating role on occasion for some smaller and middle powers—in fact a kind of a third world role before its time since this was before the influx of third world countries as from 1960.

Before 1960, at the height of the Cold War, the UN was divided into two large blocs, and it had a limited number of members from what we could call the third world. Cold War issues as well as great issues of decolonisation were debated. In that situation we had a particularly useful role to play for a period. How we, from an independent viewpoint, voted on divisive questions was then of added importance because the two blocs chose to regard their UN victories and defeats at that time as important—or at least as useful propaganda. Our support for anti-colonial resolutions were important then, even at times perhaps decisive and these resolutions themselves made a difference.

But the UN has changed. The Cold War blocs have largely dissolved; and the Great Powers have less interest. The great oppositions have died away and the Great Powers play defensive or apathetic roles. Most of the decolonisation battles have been won. Some fifty newly independent African and Asian members have joined since the early 1960s and Ireland's role as an independent member with anti-colonial sympathies is no longer unusual. These newly independent countries can and do promote most vigorously their own interests and those of the remaining colonial territories and they put forward their own resolutions on such issues as apartheid and the remaining problems of colonialism.

It is certainly true that there were issues in which we did take a very prominent role (under Frank Aiken). These were nuclear non-proliferation, 1958–1961, the strengthening of the UN peace-keeping capacity, 1960–1967. It is also true that very good 'press relations' gave public opinion at home a somewhat exaggerated view of Ireland's honourable role and this heightened view has now become accepted wisdom. The result may be today an over-sanguine view of the UN (or for that matter of the ministers of the eight European states and what Ireland has done for it or them, and what they might one day do for Ireland).

4. There then comes trade and economic benefit with the details of which we are not here really concerned but expansion and the economic programme of the Lemass and Whitaker combine were very much the order of the day and these plans and developments began to exercise a decisive change in foreign policy—one which imperceptibly but definitely brought about the re-orientation of diplomatic objectives—away from New York and on to Europe. Trade certainly led easily and naturally into the Irish application of July 1961 for admission to the EEC. It was not indeed until 22 January 1972 that Ireland signed the Treaty of Accession. Between 1961 and 1972 lay the era of de Gaulle and his persistent bar upon British and therefore incidentally and inevitably Irish accession. Our foreign policy in those years moved in close harmony to that of the United Kingdom—with whose economic interests we remained closely attached. The Anglo-Irish economic agreement prepared Ireland for some of the steps required for participation in Europe—when de Gaulle removed himself from office and the ban was lifted.

The EEC decision was courageous enough at the time; and in retrospect perhaps, and certainly at the time, seemed a considerable change of direction for a country which had built its independence on the Sinn Fein concept of economic nationalism and self-sufficiency. That decision must be most probably attributed to Lemass while Aiken remained to a substantial extent aloof, if indeed his opposition did not go further as far as actual disapproval. But Fianna Fáil knows how to keep its secrets and its internal quarrels rarely surfaced—at least until 1970 and the clash between Lynch and Haughey.

The swing away from UN was hardly noticeable until the middle 1960s; and there was little cause for disagreement, either secret or public, in government or party circles or indeed in public opinion itself. The so-called Red China controversy aroused some interest in Irish politics in the Dáil and in the correspondence columns of the *Irish Times*. The old red scare was resurrected in 1956-57. The Irish delegation, led by Frank Aiken, voted in favour of placing on the agenda of the UN the issue of the exclusion of the Chinese Communist government. It was often loosely and exaggeratedly thought that Cruise O'Brien had played the decisive part in influencing the minister for External Affairs on this point and, indeed, some evidence along these lines and in support of that interpretation was provided by Cruise O'Brien in his entrancing autobiographical piece *To Katanga and Back* : some commentators interpreted the controversy in a more personal manner. The truth is that the minister himself was in theory and in fact responsible. It was sometimes forgotten that precedent had been set on this very kind of matter by de Valera as far back as September 1934, when, at the League of Nations, he supported the admission of the Soviet Union. At this later stage Aiken was not voting for the admission of China, but only for discussion of the issue and its being placed on the agenda.

Aiken obviously acted with the full approval of the Taoiseach, but it is not so clear as to whether a government decision was actually taken on this point or whether the matter was left entirely to the discretion of the Foreign Minister. There was no real party conflict on this controversy. Liam Cosgrave had referred in a speech of December 1955 to the anomaly of the absence of the Chinese government, representing almost a quarter of the population of the universe. Within the delegation at New York there was some disagreement as to whether mention should be made of 'God' or of 'Providence'. Prudence here prevailed and the more neutral sounding term was naturally chosen.

There were probably differences of opinion about the direction of Irish foreign policy, as far as concerned the government. De Valera had retired to Aras an Uachtaráin. He was to remain quiet on foreign policy, as a general rule. But he did make some sceptical noises about Europe and the materialism for which, in his view, it partly stood. Lemass may have been his choice for the succession; but de Valera's heart beat more with that of Aiken. Lemass and Aiken each represented different strands of the Sinn Fein and the Fianna Fáil position. Lemass was more concerned with issues such as economic growth and development.

Aiken viewed his role as being primarily concerned with the continuation and development of a separate Irish foreign policy at the UN. Lemass increasingly thought in terms of London and Europe; Aiken preoccupied himself with issues raised in New York—where indeed he spent a very long time each year attending as many meetings as he could. Each of these two powerful ministers kept out of each other's way and as far as was possible left a free hand to the other.

Aiken was closer to the inner councils of the very discreet and taciturn 'chief'. Aiken indeed was not much interested in Europe. At one point he had advocated the reduction of Irish diplomatic representation in Western Europe to one single embassy. Lemass and Whitaker went to Europe on a general tour in their effort to seek admission to the EEC; Aiken said little or nothing but pursued his UN interest in peace-keeping, non-proliferation, disarmament, and new schemes for international financial co-operation. Aiken's preference for the UN represented his conception of the respective importance of the UN historical role versus that of the European.

Cardinal Spellman, of power and influence in New York, brought the row over Red China into the open in the United States, and he succeeded in mobilising some support for opposition to recognising Red China among semi-state and other economic bodies in Ireland. The Prince of the Church went so far as to threaten the boycott by Irish American Catholics of Irish Airlines and Irish tourism. One would only fly American to Lourdes in the future.

Indeed, Aer Lingus and the Tourist Board were not entirely unimpressed by the economic and financial implications of such a threat. But Aiken was hardly likely to pay any attention whatsoever to such considerations whereas Lemass again, in all probability, did. De Valera here too may have played some part. If he did, he would have understood more the mind and aspirations of the Foreign Minister.

Meanwhile, Irish foreign policy in those days was active on many matters including the issue of nuclear explosions in outer space, the financing of peace-keeping, the use for military purposes of the sea bed and other matters of concern in United Nations. Sean Ronan and Cruise O'Brien played their part as civil servants in advising their active minister on all these points.

Aiken later was to regret the departure from the Irish diplomatic service of Cruise O'Brien, however much he was to resent the publication of a book and articles by Cruise O'Brien on his experiences as a diplomatic colleague. Lemass did not, on the contrary, regret Cruise O'Brien's resignation.

Meanwhile de Valera, while he remained in office as Taoiseach, did not encourage much public discussion on any of these matters. He had come to concern himself with the problems and possibilities of the presidency and with the abolition of proportional representation. Domestic rather than international affairs were in the forefront of his thinking and planning. He therefore left foreign affairs to Aiken, whom he trusted and domestic policy to Lemass whom he respected and accepted.

The decade from 1959 to 1969 saw there the continuation of the Aiken policy at United Nations. But Irish affairs and Irish influence—for the reasons mentioned earlier—seemed to have gradually diminished. Aiken pursued his various schemes but without real success. The great and formative period of 1958 to 1962 was over and the EEC was beginning to play an ever increasing role in the actual shaping of policy. It seemed too as if Anglo-Irish relations were recovering from the disillusion and recrimination of 1949 and after. Each of the two countries had common interests and—apart from agriculture—felt the need to combine their efforts in entering Brussels. There was the indubitable and significant fact of the *Anglo-Irish Free Trade Agreement*; there was also the appearance of harmony on the political scene as regards developments in Ulster. Terence O'Neill and Sean Lemass, brought together by Kenneth Whitaker, appeared to be introducing a new era of co-operation in economic and, what was more important, political collaboration.

But that honeymoon was short-lived and in 1969 relations between Britain and Ireland took a sharp turn for the worse in relation to the breakdown of law and order throughout the Northern province. We are here, however, not concerned with the details of the Ulster situation in those years, only with its impact on international politics. The civil rights movement and the reaction to it, in particular the steady rise of violence, caused a lot of international notice. We are too close to the events to speak with any certainty as to the nature of that notice in certain countries—say for example Czechoslovakia, the United States of

America, or Eastern Germany. In these countries interest and attention went so far as to encourage the provision of arms to paramilitary forces steadily developing in the North.

The issue boiled over once into the arena of the UN in August 1969. Since Ireland had been admitted to the UN Irish delegations had frequently referred to the outstanding national problem of the unification of Ireland, particularly whenever the Irish experience of the evils of Partition seemed relevant to specific international problems under discussion. This was done a lot in the time of Aiken. It was to be continued under Dr Patrick Hillery and, indeed, Dr Garret FitzGerald was to continue the same practice.

In 1969, however, the government decided to raise formally the question of the North of Ireland at the UN. This was the first time such a course was undertaken. All other previous statements had been merely incidental. This particular decision was taken in view of the serious deterioration of the situation in the North where tension had mounted in increasing degrees from August 1968. As early as April 1969 the Irish government decided that Aiken, still Foreign Minister, should seek an immediate meeting with the Secretary General of the UN. In a press conference on 23 April after his meeting with U Thant, Aiken explained that he had come for one purpose only—namely of 'advising the Secretary General'. The Irish government 'had demonstrated,' so he said, 'that they took a serious view of the situation, also that they expected civil rights to be restored to the community in the North and an end to be put to discrimination.' This, Aiken asserted, would lead to 'eventual reunification of the country by agreement'.

This was the beginning of the rather extraordinary series of incidents and speeches which culminated in an address of an 'informal' character given by a new Foreign Minister, Patrick Hillery, who then succeeded Frank Aiken. It was Dr Hillery's first intervention on the international scene; he had been 'in' for a few weeks. Aiken had been dropped— seemingly without much notice and Hillery had little experience therefore of the stage he was now about to enter. What he wanted was permission to address the Security Council of UN 'on the Northern situation'. In a letter sent to the President of the Security Council, Jaime de Pinies of Spain, Jack Lynch, the Taoiseach, stated that, as the British government was no longer in control of the situation and the RUC was no longer accepted as an impartial police force and would not be likely to restore peaceful conditions and certainly not in the long term, the Irish government requested the British government to apply immediately to the UN for the urgent dispatch of a peace-keeping force to the Six Counties.

The British rejected that request. The Irish government then proposed there should be a joint peace-keeping force composed of members of the British and Irish defence forces. Again the British refused. The Irish government accordingly and formally appealed to the Security Council for the dispatch of a UN peace-keeping force. The Irish government meanwhile could not stand by, or so it said, also at the UN.

Relations between the British and the Irish at this stage had now almost reached their lowest level for many years. But nothing in fact was to come out of this dramatic step. Dr Hillery was new at this game but he and Cremin could not have achieved more in face of the opposition of the British government to the proposal to place Northern Ireland on the agenda, or indeed to the subsequent proposal for the establishment of a peace-keeping force. Through the good offices of Señor de Pinies, and the conciliatory behaviour of the British delegate, Lord Caradon, a compromise formula was devised. Hillery was not permitted to address a formal meeting; his motion was not put down on the agenda, but he was allowed to make a statement 'to explain why the meeting had been requested by him'. The President, Señor de Pinies, had written a short account of his presidency between August 1969 and October 1970. His comment was that the statement of the Foreign Minister of Ireland 'was very harsh, but delivered in an extremely correct manner'. The British representative found Hillery's statement was 'cautious and restrained'. He did not try to prevent the Irish delegate from making a statement, and the matter was adjourned after Caradon himself had made his own declaration. The matter was discussed on a subsequent occasion and the decision taken was recorded as follows:

The general committee decided to prepare a decision on whether or not to recommend the inclusion in the agenda of Item 102 and the Assembly during its meeting on December 20 took note of the committee's decision on that matter. The General Assembly which met on the Seventeenth of December took no further action regarding the request of the Government of Ireland.

The Spanish President himself, the Ambassador of Ireland, the Ambassador of Zambia co-operated actively with President de Pinies in acting as go-betweens; and the Soviet Union, not surprisingly, indicated its firm support for the Irish motion.

This was the first and last time that the Irish question appeared to be about to assume a central position in international affairs. It is not clear how well thought out the Irish recourse to the UN was, or how far the full and possible consequences of a UN peace-keeping force had been envisaged. There had been talk from time to time about the establishment of such a force from within the European Community itself. It is not clear also as to how far the action of the government was a response to the panic of those hot days of August 1969. Or was it partly also a device to defuse a dangerous situation? Certainly some of the protagonists involved, Hillery and Cremin, in particular, appeared to have behaved with great coolness and calming courtesy.

The situation has certainly not improved since those days and no serious effort has been made to resurrect the issue at UN. Peace-keeping may be all right for others; it may not suit us.

One aspect of foreign policy remained unchanged up to 1969 and still so remains. This is the negative attitude towards NATO. The decision of 1949 was accepted without any real demur. There was certainly no pressure from the British or the Europeans—the Americans were the most critical but even they did not show much interest. There was no need for any power to interest itself in Irish defence policy during these years. Foreign policy, in fact, was only in a very small way related to defence. In any event, our forces were so small as to be insignificant and the technology of war rendered interest in Irish bases nugatory.

By 1969 some people, as far as we know, were beginning to appreciate that adhesion to the European Community might require some modification of the policy of neutrality and might certainly involve our participation in a European defence force. Hitherto our clear policy has been that Ireland would not get involved with any military alliance but the evolution of the EEC towards a political as well as economic community might in time create a situation in which the logical corollary would be a defence community. But some held that this could only come about when agreement was reached on a common foreign policy. France, in particular, may at some point accept the logic of its position which seems to lead eventually to a European defence community. If that were so, and if we in Ireland wished to be regarded as fully European, our bluff might be called. To some extent, there was in 1969 some possibility that we might be eventually vulnerable on this issue. However, nothing that would affect our foreign policy on defence matters happened or was mentioned before 1969. We were even able to spare some troops for Africa and for Cyprus—at least until the outbreak of real crisis in our own island. The rest was pure speculation about an undisclosed future.

As from 1970, Irish diplomatic policy largely turned in the direction of Europe. Ireland was not to join the European Community until the ban on British accession had been lifted. Irish foreign policy was greatly taken up with the Northern Irish question. But this, in fact, for most politicians and parties (and of course for most civil servants following in the footsteps of their political masters) was just a great and (dangerous) nuisance. Apart from Blaney, Boland and Haughey, there were few politicians who welcomed the opportunities presented by the increasingly messy situation across the border. Bipartisanship in foreign policy was virtually achieved between the government under Jack Lynch and the main opposition parties. Admittedly, there was some talk about the possibility, for instance, of peacekeeping forces derived largely from Europe. It was known that some members of the Cabinet favoured this policy but it was not at all welcomed by the majority or by the foreign affairs advisors of the government. At the best it was to be the lesser evil, but a very bad evil at that.

FURTHER READING

R. Fanning, *The Irish Department of Finance, 1922–58*, Dublin 1978.

G. A. Hayes-McCoy, 'The Irish Defence Policy, 1938-51', in K. B. Nowlan and T. D. Williams, eds, *Ireland in the War Years and After, 1939–51*, Dublin 1969.

P. Keatinge, *The Formulation of Irish Foreign Policy*, Dublin 1973.

P. Keatinge, *A Place among the Nations: Issues of Irish Foreign Policy*, Dublin 1978.

S. F. Lemass, 'Small states in international organisations' in August Schou and Arne O. Brundtland, *Small States in International Relations*, Uppsala 1971.

N. Mansergh, *Survey of British Commonwealth Affairs: Problems of Wartime Cooperation and Post-War Change, 1939–1952*, London 1958.

N. Mansergh, 'Irish Foreign Policy, 1945–51' in K. B. Nowlan and T. D. Williams, eds, *Ireland in the War Years and After, 1939–51*, Dublin 1969.

Conor Cruise O'Brien, 'Ireland in international affairs' in Owen Dudley Edwards, ed., *Conor Cruise O'Brien introduces Ireland*, London 1969.

Northern Ireland, 1945-72

Cornelius O'Leary

The Brooke Years (1945–1963)[1]

Towards the end of World War II, the Unionist Party entered on its twenty-fifth year of continuous control in Northern Ireland. Indeed the personnel of the Cabinet had remained virtually unchanged between 1921 and Lord Craigavon's death in November 1940. However, his successor, J. M. Andrews, was ousted in 1943 by a backbench revolt and the next prime minister, the then Minister of Agriculture, Sir Basil Brooke, broadened the base of his Cabinet by including two clergymen and the former leader of the Northern Ireland Labour Party Harry Midgley.

The Stormont Parliament (elected in 1938) was dissolved on 25 May with polling on 14 June 1945. The Westminster election did not take place until 6 July. With unusual prescience the *Irish News* (23 May) claimed that the former was being held first to minimise the effect of a Labour victory in the latter. The Unionists, whose programme consisted only of the maintenance of the Union and the hope of parity in social services and economic development with Great Britain, was faced with the strongest challenge yet mounted by the Left—twenty-four Northern Ireland Labour candidates (and two Communists) claiming that the existing ministers would be unable to cope with massive post-war unemployment. Although Brooke received a fulsome eve of poll assurance from Churchill that 'in your appeal to the people of Ulster you carry with you my best wishes and the gratitude of the British race in every quarter of the globe',[2] he could scarcely have forgotten that in the worst days of the war Churchill had offered de Valera a chance of a united Ireland in return for participation in the struggle.

In the Stormont election the Unionists suffered a net loss of six seats; two Belfast seats went to NILP, two Queen's

University seats to Independents, while two border constituencies, which had been handed them through nationalist
inertia in 1938, were recovered by that party. Five Belfast seats
went to various brands of Labour—NILP, Independent Labour,
Commonwealth Labour, Socialist Republican—and the Official
Unionists were down to thirty-three seats out of fifty-two, which
though a comfortable majority was their lowest since the last election held under proportional representation, exactly twenty years
previously. In the Westminster election Jack Beattie (Independent
Labour) held West Belfast and two Nationalists were returned
again for the two-seat constituency of Tyrone-Fermanagh.
(They had abstained through the 1935–45 Parliament, but were
now authorised to attend by their constituency convention.)

The Brooke government faced two main problems in the
immediate post-war years. On the one hand, they had to work
with a Labour government commanding an overwhelming
majority at Westminster. This meant that they could be required
to pass socialist legislation distasteful to their conservative principles. As early as November 1945 the Cabinet apparently discussed the possible options.[3] Some ministers were in favour of
advocating dominion status, but that proposal was firmly
squashed by the Minister of Agriculture, the Rev. Robert Moore,
who bluntly told his colleagues that the £13 million annual
agricultural subsidies received from the British Exchequer just
could not be made good from their own taxable resources, nor
could they afford any restriction on free access to the British
market for their agricultural produce. Although, in the late
1940s, the argument for dominion status was raised again by
some Unionist backbenchers, it received no encouragement
from the Cabinet.

The policy followed by the Ulster Unionists served at the
same time to vindicate their conservatism and ensure that
Northern Ireland shared in any benefits that were going. The
great nationalisation and welfare measures introduced by the
Attlee government were consistently opposed by the Unionists
at Westminster, but when they passed into law were speedily
applied to Northern Ireland. The nationalisation measures were
of little local importance : there was no heavy industry or coal
to nationalise, while transport, gas and electricity were already
publicly owned, but the National Insurance Act 1946, the

F

National Health Act 1948 and the Education Act 1947 (a delayed follow-up of the Butler Act of 1944) were among the most socially important measures ever passed by Stormont. The first two provided for a comprehensive scheme of social insurance from all the major hazards of life and a health service 'from the cradle to the grave', with benefits and contributions at the same level as in Great Britain, while an equalisation agreement ensured that Northern Ireland would receive sufficient finance to maintain the services at the same level as in Britain. The Education Act provided for universal secondary education from the age of eleven in three types of schools. The first Act aroused little controversy but the second and third did: the Catholic authorities objected (unavailingly) to the taking over of the voluntary hospitals and the Mater Hospital in Belfast refused to come into the scheme, while some Unionists objected to the increase in the provision for buildings and maintenance of voluntary (mostly Catholic) schools, from 50 per cent (the Westminster rate) to 65 per cent, on the grounds that this was too generous to the Catholics. Both Bills, however, passed into law with only minor amendments. Another important reform was the establishment in 1945 of the Northern Ireland Housing Trust to supplement the work of local authorities; unlike the former it was never accused of discrimination. These measures ensured that in the succeeding decade the level of social services in Northern Ireland was far higher than in the Twenty-six Counties and provided in the long run an extra plank in the Unionist platform.

Two measures which caused vehement controversy pointedly demonstrated Northern Ireland's capacity for independent action. The Safeguarding of Employment Act 1947 continued the wartime practice of refusing employment to non-Ulster residents, unless it could be shown that no resident was available. Although the measure applied to migrants from England and Scotland also, its primary purpose was to prevent a flood of immigrants from south of the border, who might swell the voting ranks of the Nationalists. Its passing meant that for the first time there was a check on internal migration within the United Kingdom. The Elections and Franchise Act 1947 was important for what it did *not* contain. Although the Labour government had assimilated the parliamentary and local government franchises in

Great Britain, abolishing plural voting in both, the Stormont measure maintained the pre-war electoral structure for local government, based on rated occupation, and actually increased the possible number of business votes for a local government elector, to six. While from then until the two franchises were assimilated in 1971, the number of people on the local government register was approximately two-thirds of those entitled to the parliamentary vote (i.e. adults over twenty-one), some of those on the former had several votes! This undemocratic anomaly could be explained only by a desire to perpetuate Unionist control of local authorities in areas where they were numerically in a minority, and linked with allegations of gerrymandering was to prove a potent grievance in later decades.

Some interesting party developments occurred during these years. The Northern Ireland Labour Party (linked, though not affiliated, to the British Labour Party) seemed to make steady progress at first. In the local elections of 1947 it secured eight seats in Belfast City Council, and won control of three district councils. But since it continued its ambivalent attitude on the constitutional question (maintained since 1923) it continued as an uneasy alliance of Labour-Anti-Partitionists and Labour-Unionists. The other development was in the Nationalist ranks. Late in 1945, a new organisation, The Irish Anti-Partition League, was established to focus attention in Great Britain and the United States on 'the iniquity of partition'. Its chairman was James McSparran KC, a prominent barrister, elected for Mourne to Stormont in 1945, who had succeeded T. J. Campbell as the effective leader of the Nationalists. The Anti-Partitionists gained some support among the new Labour members at Westminster wih Irish connections —most notably Hugh Delargy and Desmond Donnelly.

The Anti-Partition cause received an unexpected boost in 1948, when de Valera after his defeat in the Dáil election of that year went on a tour of the United States, Australia, and Great Britain, 'devoting countless speeches and the whole force of his formidable personality to "Anti-Partition" '.[4] Although the reaction among Irish exiles in both parts of the world was predictably warm, the reaction in Great Britain was polite but cool. In retrospect it is difficult to see just what de Valera or the Anti-Partitionists hoped to achieve.[5] The detailed arguments they used would logically lead either to rectification of the border —since they concentrated on the fact of Nationalist majorities in the border areas—or to the elimination of discriminatory legislation in Northern Ireland, but *not* to what they regarded as the obvious conclusion, reunification of Ireland, since however one juggled the evidence one was still left with a substantial majority of Ulster voters in favour of Partition, and that was the ultimate democratic test. Again, the temper of the times was against the campaign, at least in Britain, since memories of the alleged dangers posed by Eire's neutrality during the war were still keen. Lastly, the Anti-Partition Campaign served to mask the basic inadequacies of the Nationalist Party. Since Joe Devlin's death in 1934 their leaders had been men who were successful professionally, but endowed with little political ability. Nor did they have the characteristic features of a modern democratic party—a central headquarters or regular local or constituency associations. Both in form and reality their organisation resembled that of the Irish Parliamentary Party *before* the arrival of Parnell.

The Anti-Partition Campaign reached its climax with the unexpected announcement in Canada by Costello that his government would introduce legislation to repeal the External Relations Act (September 1948) and the speedy passage of the Republic of Ireland Bill through the Oireachtas with all-party support. The Brooke government immediately sought assurances from Whitehall that this formal severance of Eire's tenuous link with the Commonwealth would not effect the constitutional position of Northern Ireland. The assurance was given, but the opportunity to make political capital was too good for the Unionists to miss. In February 1949 the Premier dissolved Stormont, asking for a massive vote 'to show the world where we stand'. The reaction of the Costello government in raising a collection (the 'Chapel Gate Collection') of £50,000 to help the Anti-Partitionist candidates was of little assistance to them (none of whom sat for a marginal constituency) but was disastrous for the NILP, all of whose seats were lost, while the Unionists got back with resounding majorities, and a net gain of four seats— the Unionist share of the vote in the contested constituencies rose from 50 per cent in 1945 to 63 per cent.

After the election the Labour Party held a special delegate

conference at which a majority finally came down on the side of the constitution, thus precipitating a split, since nearly half the membership, including ex-MPs, seceded from the Party and some joined the Irish Labour Party, which in several succeeding elections put up rival candidates against the NILP. Immediately after the formal establishment of the Republic of Ireland the Attlee government introduced the celebrated Ireland Bill, which favoured the Irish in Britain by ensuring that they would not be treated as aliens, but infuriated the Dublin government by guaranteeing the position of Northern Ireland in the United Kingdom, until the parliament of Northern Ireland should decide otherwise. The Anti-Partition Campaign continued throughout 1949 in Great Britain, but then gradually petered out.

After this excitement Northern Ireland faded from the headlines and politics reverted to the pre-war pattern of stagnation. There was virtually no opposition at Stormont, since Labour was wiped out and the Anti-Partitionists now rarely attended. Virtually the only interesting political events during these years were the results in the super-marginal Westminster constituency of West Belfast, where the veteran Jack Beattie, now standing as an Irish Labour candidate was beaten by the Rev. J. G. Mac-Manaway (Unionist) in the February election of 1950; then MacManaway was unseated by the Commons through the diligent researches of a great enemy of the Unionists, the Labour MP Geoffrey Bing;[6] in the subsequent by-election the Unionists held the seat but with a reduced majority, and in the General Election of October 1951 Beattie got back with a majority of twenty-five votes! In the Stormont election of 1953 there were twenty-five uncontested seats—the highest number since 1933—and the turnout in the contested areas fell to 61 per cent from 80 per cent in 1949. The Unionists lost one seat—Dock, which went to Irish Labour; the NILP share of the vote increased significantly but they did not win a seat.

In 1954 the IRA, which had been quiescent since the end of the war, started a new campaign with attacks on barracks in Omagh and Armagh. This republican resergence was reflected in Sinn Fein deciding to contest all the seats in the Westminster election of 1955. (They had contested three seats in 1935, none in 1945 and two in 1950.) Two candidates were elected, in

Fermanagh, South Tyrone and Mid-Ulster, but since they were already in prison for IRA activities they were unseated on petition and the seats awarded to Unionists. Sinn Fein intervention in West Belfast helped Beattie to lose the seat at his last attempt. For the first time since 1924 all the Westminster seats were held by Unionists.

Although not observed at the time, the years 1957-8 marked a watershed in Northern Ireland politics. The IRA campaign had passed its peak and internment under the Special Powers Act was having its effect; although Lord Brookeborough (Brooke had been made a peer in 1952) sought to make violence the sole issue in the Stormont election of 1958 ('reply to the bullets by our votes') the NILP won four Belfast seats; the Anti-Partition campaign was dead (McSparran retired from politics in 1958 and the Nationalist MPs elected a colourless successor) and, most important of all, at a conference in Garron Tower (County Antrim) a leading Catholic social worker, G. B. Newe urged his co-religionists to participate more in the affairs of the province. This was the first serious suggestion from within the Catholic community that acceptance of Northern Ireland *de facto* if not *de jure*, was overdue. It would be heard with increasing force in succeeding years.

The last years of Brookeborough's premiership were uneventful. In the Westminster Election of 1959 Sinn Fein again contested all the seats, but their share of the vote fell from 24 per cent to 11 per cent and the Unionists again swept all the seats. It was plain that many traditional Nationalists were abstaining rather than vote Sinn Fein. In 1962 the IRA campaign was formally called off and in the same year occurred another uneventful Stormont election: the NILP kept their four seats with increased majorities, while Nationalists won back a seat lost in 1958 to the Unionists through Republican intervention; while Dock elected a new member Gerry Fitt (Republican Labour), who was to become the best known of all non-Unionist politicians in the succeeding decade. The Unionist share of the seats went down to thirty-four.

Brookeborough continued as premier for ten months more, resigning somewhat unexpectedly on 25 March 1963, at the age of 74, after twenty years in the highest office. Right to the end he maintained his narrow, intransigent attitude. Virtually the last controversy of his premiership concerned the Irish Congress of Trade Unions, formed in 1959 through the resolution of the ancient quarrel between the two Trade Union Congresses in the Republic. Although many workers in Northern Ireland were members of all-Irish unions affiliated to the ICTU, Brookeborough resolutely refused to deal with other than British-based unions.

The O'Neill Years (1963–1969)

When Brookeborough resigned there was no machinery for electing a leader of the Unionist Party. (In this the Unionists resembled their prototype, the British Conservatives.) Constitutionally, the Governor had to designate a new Premier, and having received a report on the state of party feeling from the Chief Whip, William Craig, the Governor summoned Captain Terence O'Neill, outgoing Minister of Finance. O'Neill sprang from the same aristocratic background as his predecessor. Elected to Stormont in 1946, and holder of several ministerial posts since 1949, at the time of his appointment he was regarded as a rather undistinguished politician, in contrast to the dynamic young Minister of Home Affairs, Brian Faulkner, who also had prime ministerial ambitions. O'Neill's most significant appointment was of Faulkner as Minister of Commerce.

O'Neill's first important task was to tackle the unemployment problem. Since the war the unemployment rate in the province had run at four times the United Kingdom average. This was partly due to the release of labour from the declining manufacturing industries (especially shipbuilding and linen), partly to movement from the land and partly to a continuing high birth-rate. There had been some new industry, but the overall unemployment rate remained obstinately higher than in any other region of the United Kingdom.

The Brookeborough government had not really tried to cope with the problem, but in October 1963 the new government commissioned the distinguished Ulster-born economist, Professor Thomas Wilson, to prepare a development plan for the province. The Wilson Report (December 1964)[7] recommended the creation of 30,000 jobs in manufacturing industry over the next six years (double the previous rate) and their concentration in certain development areas, while the Belfast conurbation was to be held to a maximum of 600,000 people. The government accepted these recommendations and over the next six years Faulkner was able to secure the establishment of some sixty new factories. By 1968 the complex of six synthetic fibre factories was the greatest of its kind in the world and the Northern Ireland rate of unemployment was down to three times the United Kingdom average—a level at which it has subsequently remained. The industrial development embraced both sections of the community, and O'Neill, realising the importance of good relations with Labour, recognised the ICTU in 1964.

But O'Neill went further. In 1964 he announced that his principles were 'to make Northern Ireland prosperous and to build bridges between the two traditions in our community'. He made symbolic gestures like visiting Catholic schools—not very significant of themselves, but enough to arouse the ire of the Rev. Ian Paisley, whose formidable demagogic talents were just then being brought to public notice. The policy of conciliation made a spectacular advance with the completely unexpected visit of Lemass to Stormont in January 1965, followed by the equally record-breaking visit of O'Neill to Dublin in the following month. One gesture led to another and in February 1965 the Nationalist Party for the first time accepted the role of official opposition at Stormont, with Eddie McAteer (their leader since 1962) as Leader of the Opposition. At the end of November 1965 O'Neill precipitated a dissolution and fought the election on the £900 million development programme. Although turnout was down, there was a significant jump in the Unionist share of the vote in Belfast and two seats lost to Labour in 1958 were recaptured—including that of David Bleakley, the NILP's most articulate speaker.

But although at the end of 1965 O'Neill's position appeared stronger than any of his predecessors', he was much more vulnerable than was realised. Protestant extremists led by Paisley were continually denouncing him for 'selling out to the South', although the exchange of visits of the two Prime Ministers had no practical consequence except to promote North-South trade. However, with an overall majority of twenty seats at Stormont O'Neill could afford to ignore the Paisleyites, then unrepresented. Far more serious were two revolts within the Unionist Parliamentary Party—in 1966 and 1967—both of which O'Neill quelled by the expedient of broadcasting to the people and challenging his opponents to put their case publicly. This they were unwilling to do, and both revolts ended in votes of confidence of specious unanimity for O'Neill.

In his posthumous memoirs,[8] Brian Faulkner revealed that on the first of these occasions the rebels amounted to one less than a majority of the parliamentary party, but neither he nor any other Unionist insider has publicly acknowledged the grounds for the most disruptive move in Unionist politics since the overthrow of Andrews by Brooke in 1943. Inferentially the reasons for the intra-party opposition seemed to be akin to those of Paisley—that O'Neill was going too far in cultivating the Northern minority and the Southern government.

Throughout his troubled premiership there was strong evidence that O'Neill was winning the support of middle-class Catholics. It was nevertheless among the Catholic minority that the events were set in train that led to his downfall. There were two main causes, one economic, the other political. Though conflated in much subsequent writing, they were in origin quite distinct.

The economic development of the 1960s, as Brian Faulkner, its architect, unceasingly claimed, certainly involved both sections of the community. But that development was largely concentrated in the area east of the River Bann, the traditional heartland of Ulster industry, where the religious distribution was roughly the same as in Belfast—three-quarters Protestant to a quarter Catholic. In the area west of the Bann, where the two groups were of roughly equal size the industrial boom did not penetrate. Of fifty-eight new factories only eight went to West Ulster, and in the crucial year 1968, when the level of unemployment in the province was 7.2 per cent, in West Ulster it reached 12.6 per cent, while the predominately Catholic Derry (13.9 per cent) and Strabane (18.2 per cent) were particularly hit. The resentment obviously felt at missing out on the general prosperity was heightened by two decisions which from any objective point of view seemed indefensible—the location of the new town (Craigavon) in a densely populated area of County Armagh and the siting of the second university not in Derry with its long tradition of higher education but in the small market town of Coleraine.

The political cause was the formation of the Northern Ireland

Civil Rights Association (NICRA) in January 1967. This pressure group, largely though not exclusively Catholic, was established to agitate for uniform treatment of Ulster with the rest of the United Kingdom, especially in relation to the local government franchise, the allocation of public housing, and the rectification of local boundaries. As has been mentioned above, all these served to perpetuate Unionist control at the local level. Derry was the outstanding example, but Omagh, Armagh, and Dungannon had also had nationalist majorities before the setting up of Northern Ireland. The fact that the Nationalists controlled only eight out of the sixty-eight local authorities, and none more important than an urban district council told its own tale.

Although all these charges had often previously been made, this was the first time that they were not subsumed in a general anti-partitionist argument. The tactics of NICRA were to claim the rights of *British* subjects for all in Northern Ireland and they quickly secured the help of some young Labour MPs at Westminster, who were disgusted by the anomalies.

This was the background to the events of the summer of 1968. A civil rights march organised in Dungannon (24 August) to protest against a particularly blatant decision by the local council was met by a hostile crowd of 'Protestant Volunteers', and a confrontation was narrowly avoided by police action. On 5 October in Derry a similar march led to the famous baton charge by the RUC which television brought to the attention of the world. The 'troubles' had begun.

1968–72

Events since 1968 in Northern Ireland are so well known that it is unnecessary to attempt even a brief résumé, since for this period, unlike any other, there is a superfluity of sources. (One recent bibliography lists seven hundred items!)[9] Just a few general points need to be made.

After October 1968 O'Neill tried to reform the political system from within by conceding virtually all the civil rights demands. But his efforts were sabotaged by his own right wing, which actually held him responsible for the troubles. After another attempt to remove him from the leadership in January 1969, O'Neill called a Stormont election in which he took the extremely risky course of running 'pro-O'Neill' unionists against official party nominees whom he did not trust. The gamble failed.[10] Although the professed pro-O'Neillites scored 46 per cent of the votes in the forty-five contested seats—the highest number of contests since 1925—none of the leading anti-O'Neillites was beaten and after the election they continued their campaign, winning over some newly elected MPs. Within two months of the election O'Neill resigned and in the election for leader of the party confined to all the members of parliament —the first of its kind—O'Neill gave his own vote to the respectable, though undistinguished, Major James Chichester-Clark to keep Brian Faulkner (whom he partly blamed for his downfall) out of the premiership.

It was during Chichester-Clark's government (April 1969–March 1971) that the problem of violence became acute, with the eruption of sectarian rioting in Derry and Belfast in the week 10–16 August 1969, followed by the active intervention of the British government: the Home Secretary, James Callaghan, gradually took over responsibility for security. Under persistent pressure from Westminster the government set in train numerous reforms—including the abolition of the Special Constabulary and (at last) the assimilation of the local government and parliamentary franchises. The main opposition, now regrouped as the Social Democratic and Labour Party (founded in 1970 with Gerry Fitt as leader), accepted the seriousness of Unionist efforts, which were continued after the Conservatives returned to power in June 1970. Unfortunately, the spectre of violence raised in 1969 proved impossible to exorcise. The 'Provisional' IRA formed after a split in the movement in December 1969 proved the most extreme and durable manifestation of that body, and helped by arms from the United States started a campaign of bombing and arson in 1971 which led to repressive measures and (as expected) the withdrawal of all Catholic members from Stormont in July 1971.

Then Faulkner, who had succeeded Chichester-Clark in March 1971, made the fatal mistake of reintroducing internment on 9 August 1971. For the first time since 1921 this tactic proved counter-productive. Although hundreds were incarcerated in Long Kesh, the technological resources of modern terrorism were not easily exhausted. All the indicators of violence, murders, injuries, damage to property, soared during the last quarter of 1971 and the first of 1972—25 were killed in 1970, 173 in 1971—and led directly to the suspension of Stormont and the introduction of 'direct rule', under the first Secretary of State for Northern Ireland, William Whitelaw on 30 March 1972. The long-expected 'loyalist back-lash', in the form of the obscure Ulster Volunteer Force (founded probably in 1966) and the much more significant Ulster Defence Association (founded in September 1971) provided the final ingredients of the explosive mix that has passed for politics in the Northern Ireland of the 1970s.

Conclusion

At the beginning of this period Northern Ireland was of no more interest to students of politics or international relations than the Channel Islands or the Isle of Man. At the end, it was universally regarded as one of the world's trouble spots, like Cyprus or the Lebanon.

In recent years political scientists have devised the term 'consociational democracy' to identify countries with deep cleavages in social structure in addition to those arising from socio-economic difference, cleavages based on broad ideological or religious foundations. Empirical studies of some of these countries (e.g. Austria, Switzerland and the Netherlands) show that even where the social conditions appear unpromising, democracy can work, provided the élites concerned are prepared to co-operate. There is no uniform pattern of accommodation: it may be a permanent coalition (as in Switzerland), or a small extra-constitutional committee (as in Austria), or powerful advisory councils, as in the Netherlands. As Arendt Lijphart (the author of the term) writes: 'The essential characteristic of consociational democracy is not so much any particular institutional arrangement as the deliberate joint effort by the élites to stabilise the system.'[11]

Such accommodation in Ulster terms would mean co-operation between elected representatives of the two communities, a development which has never yet occurred—the accommodation of 1974 (the 'power-sharing' executive) involved only *half* the Protestant/Unionist élite. But as time passes it may be perceived to be inevitable, 'if passionate men are to escape being locked in an encounter of mutual frustration'.

NOTES

1. For general treatment of Northern Ireland politics before 1968, virtually the only sources are N. Mansergh, *The Government of Northern Ireland*, London, 1936, T. Wilson ed., *Ulster under Home Rule*, London, 1954 and R. J. Lawrence, *The Government of Northern Ireland*, Oxford, 1965. See C. O'Leary, 'Northern Ireland : the Politics of Illusion', *Political Quarterly*, July, 1969.
2. *Belfast News-Letter*, 13 June, 1945.
3. See the illuminating article by D. W. Harkness on the Cabinet papers of these years, *Irish Times*, 16 November, 1977.
4. F .S. L. Lyons, *Ireland since the Famine*, London, 1971, 580.
5. See B. Inglis, *West Briton*, London, 1962.
6. Bing ascertained that an Act of 1802 debarring ordained priests of the Church of England (passed specifically to exclude the 'radical parson', Rev. Horne Tooke) also applied to the Church of Ireland, since the two were united by the Act of Union 1801.
7. *Economic Development in Northern Ireland* (Cmd. 479), 1965.
8. B. Faulkner, *Memoirs of a Statesman*, ed. J. Houston, London 1978, 40–41.
9. J. Darby, *Conflict in Northern Ireland: the Development of a Polarised Community*, Dublin, 1976.
10. See C. O'Leary, 'The Northern Ireland General Election of 1969', *Verfassung und Verfassungswirklichkeit. Jahrbuch 1969*, Cologne, 1969, 123–136.
11. A. Lijphart in K. McRae ed., *Consociational Democracy* Carleton : Toronto, 1974, 76.

Continuity and Change in Ireland, 1945-70

J. J. Lee

There seems to be general agreement among contributors to this volume that the 1960s marked some sort of watershed in Irish history. This appears to be one of those pivotal periods when a society swings on its axis to face in a new direction. The contributors have singled out the 1960s as a seminal decade across a whole range of Irish experience, political, economic, educational, legal, religious, and, though perhaps more ambiguously, cultural. The years from 1945 to about 1960 appear, from this perspective as an epilogue to a traditional Ireland on the verge of extinction. To establish the essence of this 'traditional' Ireland we must delve back well before 1945.

Tradition is an elusive concept. It is tempting to think of it as somehow stretching back to time immemorial. But many apparently 'timeless' traditions spring into existence at particular moments, to satisfy the self-images and interests of particular groups. Many of the values associated with the 'traditional' Ireland that was to be buried in the 1960s stretched back no more than a century. Many were the immediate product of the great famine of 1845–50. The famine marked a dramatic shift in the power-structure of Irish society. The farming classes were suddenly relieved, by a providential stroke, from the incubus of the far more numerous, and frequently hostile, labourers and cottiers. The farming classes were now free to impose their own values on society at large. Making all due allowance for variations within the farming community, these values sanctified the primacy of property in the rural status system.

In order to pass on the farm intact, the father had generally to ensure that only two children married locally, the son who inherited the farm, and the daughter who would marry into a neighbouring farm or into a shop, whose assets had been

sedulously investigated. Other children had to be largely disinherited. Children who chose to stay at home could not marry
within the rural status system. They could usually survive only
as 'relatives assisting', to linger through life, half indulged, half
despised, as the maiden aunt and uncle, members of that legion
of stunted personalities scattered throughout rural Ireland,
where wealth accumulated and 'relatives assisting' decayed.

This system inevitably fostered family tensions. It could
flourish only as long as emigration served as a lightning con-
ductor for potential conflict. Emigration was a prerequisite for
the effective functioning of the inheritance system within the
farming class. It served too as an indispensable antidote to class
tensions, so acute before the famine, between farmers and
labourers. Emigration was the foundation on which the viability
of the new 'traditional' society rested. Rural Ireland became
after the famine an increasingly hard, calculating, materialistic
society, riven by potentially bitter internal tensions. The winners
in the famine stakes had to legitimise their victory by manufacturing integrationist traditions that would reconcile the disinherited
to their fate, whether the disinherited class, the agricultural
labourers, or the disinherited children within the farm family,
or even what one might call with scant exaggeration, the disinherited sex, women, who lost the independent income, however
meagre, they enjoyed from the domestic industry that received
its final death blow in the famine. Wives subsequently had to
become generally more subservient to their domestic masters,
their husbands, as had the growing proportion of women who
could now never marry, and who lived largely in economic depen-
dence on their fathers or brothers. The appropriate 'traditions'
were duly manufactured to draw a decorous veil over the ugly
face of Irish materialism. Ideologies of illusion provided the
bond to reconcile rhetoric with reality by focussing initially on
the role of the family, the role of women, and the role of sex.
Later, they would broaden out into the role of the race and
nation.

It was no coincidence that the family came to be idealised
ideologically at the very moment when Irish parents were scatter-
ing their children in a manner unprecedented in Irish history
by driving them into emigration. The emphasis on the sanctity
of the family as the fundamental unit of society played a crucial

role in the self-deception essential to the new tradition. Pre-famine ideology laid much less stress on the role of the family, partly because the family enjoyed a more cohesive existence than in post-famine Ireland. It was inconceivable that the parents in such idealised families should actually expel their own children from cold mercenary calculation, however unconsciously. Emigrants had therefore to be regularly romanticised as 'exiles' in an orgy of mass self-deception, which reached its apotheosis in the 'exiled children abroad' of the Proclamation of the Republic. The landlord had to be demonologised as the evil genius forcing the dissolution of the farm family—at the moment when his power began to crumble. Simultaneously, as it could not be admitted that the farmer himself had been the target for much of the agrarian outrage perpetuated by indignant labourers before the famine, this endemic feature of an earlier traditional Ireland had to be obliterated from the collective memory.

Just at the moment when women were losing a good deal of such independence as they enjoyed, their role came to be idealised. Womanhood came to be equated with motherhood at precisely the period when a higher proportion of Irish girls than ever before, or than in any other European country, were beginning to be denied the chance of motherhood in Ireland by the working of the ruthlessly materialistic marriage market.

The obsessive equation of sex with sin was another disting-uishing feature of the 'traditional' ideology invented after the famine. It was largely alien to existing Irish traditions, and was indeed partly imported from Victorian England. It helped reconcile the disinherited to their celibacy if they remained at home instead of emigrating, and ensured that inheritance pat-terns would not be spoiled by untimely 'accidents' occurring due to the delayed age of marriage. It therefore protected the in-heritance system of the farmer, whose children dominated the clergies which preached these necessary values.

The preoccupation with sex, the virtual equation of immor-ality with sexual immorality, conveniently diverted attention from less remunerative features of christian doctrine. It was as if the intensity of the concentration on sexual morality was thought to compensate for a more relaxed concept of other moralities. The morality of deceit in commercial and legal transactions, the morality of perjury, the morality of violence, were all relegated to reassuringly venial status in the hierarchy of moralities. Drunkenness was even translated into the weakness of 'the good man'. Statistical evidence suggests that the number of 'good men' increased alarmingly as the disinherited sought spiritual solace, or so some would argue, in the main internal migration route, the bottle. A compulsive concentration on a morality shrivelled to sexual morality became a distinguishing feature of the new 'traditional' catholicism of post-famine Ireland.

'Traditional' Ireland relied for its survival on a human haemorrhage. The prevailing marriage, money and morality nexus depended on it. But if the haemorrhage became too severe, the patient would either wither away or demand a drastic change of treatment. In the first fifteen years after the World War II the haemorrhage got out of control. More than 500,000 people abandoned their 'traditional' Ireland between 1945 and 1961 as the wave of emigration surged forward. In 1957 a brilliant Irish-American scholar could wonder if Ireland was to become the first nation in history destined to disappear through 'an implosion upon a central vacuity'[1] or, put more colloquially, if Ireland was going to disappear down its own plug-hole. The crisis of 'traditional' Ireland in the 1950s threw down the gauntlet to a new generation. It remained to be seen if any were left who could rise to the challenge. The answer came with almost dramatic suddenness, symbolised and personified by the rise to political and administrative leadership of Sean Lemass and T. K. Whitaker.

'Traditional' Ireland had found its noblest personification in Eamon de Valera, whose capacity for heroic self-deception concerning social realities verged on genius. This society, however distorted its self-image, could nevertheless inspire great dedication in the service of its spiritual ideals, sacred or secular, among those unconscious of its materialistic basis. Mr de Valera's Constitution of 1937 ironically codified the 'traditional' values at a moment when post-famine society could be seen to be already doomed by its own innate sterility. It would be melodramatic to claim that 'traditional' Ireland is dead and gone, with de Valera in the grave, though the arcadian Ireland of his dreams would be now buried for ever, had it ever existed. The façade of de Valera's Ireland was already crumbling before his departure because the foundations were rotting. Only the majesty of the man himself concealed some of the worst fissures in the edifice. The challenge confronting his successor when de Valera resigned in 1959 was whether he could build a new society on the ruins of the old. It was to be the historic achievement of Sean Lemass to lay the foundations of a new Ireland, perhaps destined to endure as long as its immediate predecessor.

De Valera's style was unique. He could leave no successor in his own image. The more glaring the contrast between himself and his successor the greater the likelihood of that successor leaving his own distinctive mark. The contrast between de Valera and Lemass was not one primarily between idealism and pragmatism. Lemass was as idealistic in his vision as de Valera, de Valera as pragmatic a party manager and tactician as Lemass. The contrast was one between illusionist and realist, not between idealist and pragmatist. Millions would never dwell in the house de Valera shaped in his heart, because it was built on illusory foundations, however noble the design. The realism of Lemass, on the other hand, was not that of 'the lawyers who sat in council, the men with the keen long faces', but the realism of the idealist devoted to the reality rather than to the rhetoric of his ideals. Lemass despised a national personality cult nursing itself on infantile fantasies, cowering from the challenge of self-knowledge. Growing up involved above all the substitute of reality for fantasy, a willingness to subject one's own assumptions to constant scrutiny. It was this refusal to shirk self-examination that proved so subversive to 'traditional' values, dependent as they were on a fundamental self-deception.

Lemass was fortunate that the crisis of the 1950s brought to the helm of the Department of Finance the young T. K. Whitaker. His appointment as Secretary of the Department in 1956 over the heads of more senior officials reflected the desperation of the situation. The story of the economic recovery following the first Programme for Economic Expansion in 1958 has often been recited. Two general features deserve particular emphasis. Firstly, Whitaker may not have been originally appointed to plan for expansion, but rather to pursue a rigorous policy of retrenchment. But he had the calibre of mind to re-examine his assumptions in the light of changing circumstances. Whitaker shared with Lemass a willingness to revise his attitude in the face of fresh evidence. It was this capacity to think through first principles which, allied with their energy, ability and patriotism, made the partnership of Lemass and Whitaker so fruitful. Secondly, at the institutional level, the commitment of the Department of Finance to expansionist economic policies was itself revolutionary in the context of Irish governance. Expansionist ideals, insofar as they had existed at all, had hitherto been associated mainly with the Department of Industry and Commerce, which had to fight a regular war of attrition against the Department of Finance.[2] That the premier department should now commit itself to expansion, and expansion through planning at that, marked a historic change in the history of the state.

A commitment to planning for expansion involved a new emphasis on information. The quest for knowledge therefore assumed unprecedented importance during the 1960s. Serious research into the nature of Irish society began for the first time on a sustained basis. There were now at least some who were no longer scared to look at themselves, warts and all, or terrified, however subconsciously, at the threat of truth. The role of the Central Statistics Office became crucial with the growing demand for knowledge. It was fortunate to enjoy the leadership of two gifted directors, Dr R. C. Geary and Dr M. D. McCarthy, under whose guidance it rose to the challenge of change and supplied the statistics that provided the hard cutting edge to the policy recommendations of the growing number of intellectually impressive enquiries. The Economic and Social Research Institute was established in 1960 to supply systematic analysis of economic conditions. It reflected on the dearth of suitably qualified people in the country forty years after independence that a high proportion of the early staff had to be imported. 'Traditional' Ireland had not encouraged socio-economic enquiry.

The importance of knowledge involved a new emphasis on education. The role of education assumed rapidly increasing importance in government thinking, and in public opinion, in a remarkably short period. 'In 1956 the . . . Government was able to reduce the secondary school per capita grant by 10 per cent without a loss of protest—even from the secondary schools. At the time there was no realisation of the importance of education in the modern world and there was certainly no evidence of this outburst of enthusiasm for education which is so characteristic now.'[3] The report entitled *Investment in Education*, which was published in 1965 following an enquiry under the chairmanship of Patrick Lynch, ranks as one of the fundamental intellectual and moral contributions to the making of a new Ireland. It banished once and for all the complacent banalities of 'traditional' educational thought. A Commission on Higher Education—the first in the history of the state, which itself is eloquent testimony to traditional priorities—was set up in 1960, under the chairmanship of Cearbhaill O'Dálaigh. Many recommendations of the Commission, which reported in 1967, were not implemented. But the responsibility imposed on the universities of appraising their own performance proved a salutary experience, and helped initiate rather significant changes in university standards and mentalities.

The civil service itself did not remain immune from searching scrutiny. The Devlin Commission, the first to investigate it since the Brennan Commission of 1932–5, reported in 1969. The contrast between the controversial, sometimes wrong-headed, but always intellectually stimulating Devlin Report, and the uncontroversial but intellectually contemptible Brennan Report, neatly symbolises the gulf separating the new Ireland from the old. Devlin's recommendations were implemented no more rapidly than O'Dálaigh's.

Nevertheless, however exasperatingly slow change in the civil service and in the universities may have seemed to the more impatient enthusiasts, and however egregious some of their decision-making procedures may still seem to be, they both probably changed more rapidly in a decade than in the previous century.

The diffusion of information also acquired a new significance in the 1960s. The quality of radio and of journalism improved in many respects. Garret Fitzgerald, at first virtually single-handed, was already pioneering in the 1950s, as 'analyst' of the *Irish Times*, a new level of sophistication in public economic comment. Television exercised a pervasive influence. The state had 438,000 TV licences on 31 December 1970 compared with only 93,000 on 31 March 1962.[4] The fact that the opening of an Irish television station coincided with the spread of a questioning mentality and a receptivity to change among the public increased its potential influence further. Television helped promote a capacity for self-criticism by asking awkward questions, pulling back the edges of carpets, exposing feet of clay. It also acted, however, as a major conduit of imported mass cultural influences. Over 50 per cent of RTE television broadcasting featured imported programmes at the end of the 1960s. In 1971 nearly 90 per cent of children's programmes were imported.[5] When combined with the impact of British television, which could be viewed along the east coast, this probably did more in a decade to anglicise, or to anglo-Americanise, Irish popular culture than the official anglicisation policies of centuries of British government.

Change rather than continuity appears then as the dominant motif running through the 1960s. With growing industrialisation and urbanisation, the value system of the strong farmer began to lose its grip on Irish society. 'Relatives assisting' and agricultural labourers now virtually vanished as occupational categories. The disinherited in Irish society had long been voting with their feet. 'Independence' had not meant independence for them. The 'fight for freedom' had merely ensured their continuing freedom to emigrate. Town-country tensions began to emerge effectively for the first time. So too, in reaction, did farmer organisations. The very fact that farmers felt it necessary to organise in pressure groups reflected their changing role in society. Organisation must substitute for ideology. The farming organisations were effectively led, but it is symptomatic of changing values that they felt obliged to pitch their arguments in the economic terminology of the new tradition instead of remaining content to rest their case on the axiomatic moral superiority of an ideal rural social order.

'Its success or failure will be measured by the emigration figures' predicted a leader writer of the first Programme for Economic Expansion.[6] The emigration figures, however, provide a clue to much more than merely economic trends. The stability of 'traditional' Ireland depended so intimately on emigration that the fall in the figures throughout the 1960s sounded the death knell of 'traditional' society. Emigration subsided from a flood to a trickle in what was, in historic terms, a spectacular change of trend. And as the material base of post-famine society was eroded, the corresponding ideologies of illusion began to crumble.

Marriage rates in the 1960s rose rapidly for the first time in a century, and couples also began to marry at a younger average age. The Irish changed from being one of the oldest to one of the youngest peoples in Europe. 'Traditional' Ireland, which had prattled so loudly about the 'family', had conspicuously failed to match words with deeds. The number of families increased by an annual average of only 800 between 1946 and 1961. Between 1961 and 1971 it rose at an annual average of 5,000.[7]

The nature of the family, and in particular the role of the woman in the family, was likely to change with the dramatic turnabout in the economy from sustained stagnation to sustained growth. New opportunities of fulfilling careers began to emerge for intelligent women. An increasing number of women, and men, particularly in the younger age group, began to question the equation of womanhood with motherhood, or at least with interminable childbearing. Evidence accumulated throughout the 1960s that birth control within marriage, by whatever means, was becoming increasingly widespread among the younger generation. This fundamental shift in attitude may have begun to change the daily life styles of more Irish women than any other single development since the famine.

Change, even fundamental change, does not necessarily involve the sudden submergence of old landmarks beneath an all-engulfing tide. It often involves a displacement of one generation by another, with the values of the older generation lingering on until time takes its toll. Many elements of continuity remained throughout the 1960s. They were most noticeable at the institutional level, particularly in religion and in politics.

The Catholic Church continued to command the religious allegiance of the vast majority of the southern Irish. The nature of Catholicism, however, changed somewhat. 'Traditional' Irish Catholicism had been created very quickly after the famine, partly to satisfy the requirements of the new strong farmer élite. As usually happens, the doctrinal emphases that were partly the product of a momentary conjunction of circumstances, assumed in the eyes of the faithful of later generations an authority based on the assumption that they stretched back to the very dawn of christianity. The changes associated with the Second Vatican Council therefore came as a tremendous shock to many clergy and laity. In the circumstances, the Catholic hierarchy navigated a skilful course through the 1960s. Several senior clergymen continued to regard the Council as more a threat than a promise. They, in turn, were subjected to severe criticism from the more impatient advocates of ecumenicism and renewal. The Church had to cater for all its flock, however, not merely for conservatives alone or for progressives alone. Those Catholics who equated ritual with religion suffered severe trauma. Many Catholics, and presumably many pious mothers in particular, felt deeply afflicted by the different, and to them incomprehensible, attitudes of their children towards the role of ritual in religion and of religion in society. Churches must take cognisance of all generations, not just of the younger ones pressing most urgently for change, sometimes with scant regard for the susceptibilities and vulnerability of the elders. The cautious, but not reactionary, course charted by the episcopal helmsmen, guided by a shrewd judge and congenial consensus figure in Cardinal Conway, may have been a more important factor than is sometimes allowed in helping Irish society adjust to the pressures of change, indirectly in secular as well as directly in religious matters. The Church continued to provide psychic moorings for many who might otherwise have suffered a good deal more emotional disturbance in the face of incomprehensible change. If clerical concepts of morality still retained the traditional preoccupation with sexual morality, a growing concern for a broader concept of morality can be detected during the period.

Fianna Fáil and Fine Gael continued to dominate the political landscape, following the ignominious demise of Clann na Poblachta and Clann na Talún. The continuity was, however, deceptive in several respects. The brand names remained the same, but the quality of the product changed. The consolidation of the new Fianna Fáil in the 1960s after the uninspired performance of the party between 1945 and 1957 was the major party political achievement of the whole period. And the party proved bigger than its leaders, however much it owed to them. It shrugged off the departure of its revered Chief in 1959. The new leadership cadre created by Lemass survived equally successfully his own departure in 1966, with Jack Lynch proving an outstanding electoral performer. Lynch's general election triumph in 1969 had a special significance. Lynch was the first Fianna Fáil leader who had not been directly involved in the struggle for independence. He couldn't even claim an appropriate pedigree. He was himself conscious—perhaps too conscious —of his lack of republican roots. Not all his followers considered the camán an adequately virile substitute for the gun. The lesson of the 1969 election was that in the country, if not necessarily in certain circles in the party, he could inspire other loyalties and appeal to the people over the heads of some of his colleagues. It is doubtful if Lynch could have pursued his course so grittily through the harrowing years of the party infighting after 1969 but for this electoral success.

Fine Gael's opening to the Left, in the guise of the Just Society programme, helped paradoxically to ensure that Irish politics would not develop into a Left versus Right confrontation. Fine Gael, whether under James Dillon or Liam Cosgrave, was bound to remain in large measure, in view of the sources of its electoral support, a conservative party. Declan Costello might give Fine Gael a left wing but he could not make Fine Gael a left wing party. Of the two major parties, only Fianna Fáil, which had once flirted with radicalism, at least by Irish standards, could just possibly reconstruct itself as a left wing movement. It indulged no such death wish. A Fianna Fáil opening to the left might have led to a left-right re-alignment; a Fine Gael opening to the left could not, at least in the 1960s. On the contrary, it merely ensured that both Fianna Fáil and Fine Gael would remain essentially coalitions of interest groups spanning the narrow Irish ideological spectrum. Labour's belated attempt to present itself in the guise of a genuinely socialist alternative failed to achieve significant electoral success, and left the party in as ineffectual a position in 1970 as in 1960.

Elements of continuity survived prominently in other areas too. The scale of society remained small, indeed minute. Impersonal meritocratic criteria collided with hallowed promotional criteria of consanguinity and seniority. The guardians of traditional values in the public service, the universities, trade unions, and business mounted a stern defence. Nevertheless, they were fighting an essentially losing battle, however protracted the resistance they might maintain. The corruption of mediocrity remained widespread, but no longer all-pervasive. Merit became an increasingly prevalent criterion of promotion in the public service, as well as in the universities, however tardy the rate of progress might appear to the more impatient spirits, and however gross the injustices inflicted on victimised individuals.

Many of those who did well out of 'traditional' Ireland, and who could contemplate with unruffled composure the crisis of the 1950s—a crisis in many ways attributable to their own mediocrity of mind—may remain sceptical about either the degree or the desirability of the changes of the 1960s. But the generation that grew to manhood in the 1950s and faced the bleak choice between emigrating or vegetating in a dead-end society harbours little doubt about the measure of the achievement. Not even the most committed crusaders for change would claim, however, that all the results were equally attractive. Lemass liked to argue that a rising tide rises all boats. That wasn't entirely true. Much residual poverty remained. Inevitably, some scum floated to the top as well. Materialism was hardly more rampant in the Ireland of the 1960s than in 'traditional' Ireland, but it became more blatant. A hint of the rat race syndrome could be clearly detected. That wasn't, insofar as the historian can judge, on the basis of inevitably impressionistic evidence, because there were more rats around. 'Traditional' Ireland was crawling with rats. They just couldn't race. Despite therefore the persistence of certain 'traditional' features it seems probable that the 1960s will continue to be seen, as it has been throughout this volume, as a pivotal decade in the history of modern Irish society.

NOTES

1. John Kelleher, 'Ireland : Where Does She Stand?', *Foreign Affairs*, 1957, 495.
2. This emerges clearly from Ronan Fanning, *The Irish Department of Finance 1922–58*, Dublin, 1978.
3. Sean Lemass Looks Back, *Irish Press*, 4 February 1969, 9.
4. *Statistical Abstract*, 1965, 316; 1970–71, 334.
5. *Statistical Abstract*, 1970–71, 334.
6. *Irish Times*, 12 November 1958.
7. Calculated from *Statistical Abstract*, 1955, 29; 1970–71, 40; 1972–73, 46.

Contributors

Biographical Details

Brendan Clarke, who holds a senior position in An Foras Forbartha, was born in Dublin. A former tutor in History at University College, Dublin, a former chairman of the Irish Committee for Justice and Peace, and a member of the International Affairs Committee of the Royal Irish Academy, he has written and broadcast on a wide range of current affairs.

Douglas Gageby, editor of *The Irish Times*, was born in Dublin. After serving in the national army he became a journalist in 1945, and has contributed frequently to radio and television programmes.

J. J. Lee, Professor of Modern History, University College, Cork, was born in Tralee, Co. Kerry. He has held posts in the Department of Finance, Dublin, University College, Dublin and Peterhouse, Cambridge. His publications include *The Modernisation of Irish Society, 1848–1918* (Gill and Macmillan 1973) and numerous articles on Irish and German history.

Bryan M. E. McMahon, Professor of Law, University College, Cork, was born in Listowel, Co. Kerry. He has practised law in the USA and has been a Stagaire Professor with the Council of Europe in Strasbourg. His publications include *Irish Economic Law* (EEC Commission), *Occupiers' Liability in Ireland: Survey and Proposals for Reform* (Government Publications Prl. 4403), and numerous articles and reports on legal matters.

Maurice Manning, lecturer in Politics, University College, Dublin, was born in Bagenalstown, Co. Carlow. He is chairman of the Irish Association for European Studies, and a member of the Executive of the Committee of Cooperation for European Parliamentary Studies. His publications include *The Blueshirts* (Gill and Macmillan 1971), *Irish Political Parties—An Introduction* (Gill and Macmillan 1972) and contributions to H. R. Penniman, ed., *Ireland at the Polls* (Washington, D.C. 1978).

John A. Murphy, Professor of Irish History, University College, Cork, was born in Macroom, Co. Cork. He has represented the National University of Ireland constituency in Seanad Eireann since 1977, and was Distinguished Visiting Professor at James Madison University, Harrisonburg, Virginia in 1979. His publications include *Ireland in the Twentieth Century* (Gill and Macmillan 1975) and numerous articles on Irish history.

Cornelius O'Leary, Reader in Political Science, The Queen's University, Belfast, was born in Newcastlewest, Co. Limerick. His publications include *Irish Elections 1918–77: parties, voters and Proportional Representation* (Gill and Macmillan 1979), and (with Ian Budge), *Belfast: Approach to Crisis. A Study of Belfast Politics, 1613–1970* (London 1973) as well as numerous articles on Irish, Ulster and British politics.

Gearóid Ó Tuathaigh, lecturer in History, University College, Galway, was born in Limerick. A regular contributor in both Irish and English to RTE radio and television, he has also lectured extensively in Britain and the USA. His publications include *Ireland before the Famine, 1798–1848* (Gill and Macmillan 1972) and numerous articles on Irish history.

John Pratschke, lecturer in Applied Economics, University College, Galway, was born in Cobh, Co. Cork. He has held posts in the Economic and Social Research Institute, Dublin; the University of Waterloo, Ontario, Canada; the Central Bank, Dublin; and the Statistical Office of the European Communities in Luxembourg. He has published monographs and articles in Ireland, the USA and Europe.

John Sheehan, lecturer in Economics, University College, Dublin, was born in Waterford. He has taken a special interest in the economics of education, on which he has published widely, and has acted as expert consultant for the NIEC and the NESC.

Brendan Walsh, Research Professor, Economic and Social Research Institute, Dublin, was born in Dublin. He has held posts in the USA and in Iran, and has contributed numerous papers to the Institute's publication series on a wide range of economic and social issues.

John H. Whyte, Reader in Political Science, The Queen's University, Belfast, was born in Malaya. He has held posts at Makarere University and University College, Dublin. His publications include *The Independent Irish Party, 1850–1859* (1958), *Church and State in Modern Ireland, 1923–70* (Gill and Macmillan 1971) and numerous articles on Irish and comparative political and religious history.

T. Desmond Williams, Professor of Modern History, University College, Dublin, was born in Dublin. He was a founding editor of the *Cambridge Journal* in 1947, editor of Historical Studies, Vols I and VIII (1958, 1971), and editor of *The Irish Struggle, 1916–1926* (London 1966). He was also co-editor (with R. Dudley Edwards) of *The Great Famine* (Dublin 1956) and (with Kevin B. Nowlan) of *Ireland in the War Years and After, 1938–51* (Gill and Macmillan 1969). He has published numerous articles on Irish and European history.

Index